JEREMIA VAN, PH.D.

Too Humble Too Long

Goals in Motion: A Female Soldier's Story

Contents

Foreword

This book outlines my journey from when I realized that I was going to the Army to the time I began to understand my purpose in the Army. In retrospect, I started out at the Private First Class (PFC) rank and became a Lieutenant Colonel (LTC) with a Ph.D. I hope my journey inspires anyone who has been told at every turn that what they want to accomplish is impossible. Challenges and obstacles may come, but they do not always last. If a challenge or obstacle exists, then so does one's determination. The color of your skin is not a setback. Your gender is not a setback. Where you grew up is not a setback. Your family's status in the community, or lack thereof, is not a setback. Your level of education is not a setback. Your disability is not a setback. Whatever you deemed a setback, obstacle, or challenge, God meant for your good. That is what makes your accomplishments so great in the end.

Along my journey, I learned to believe in myself. I learned to be kind to myself. I learned to give myself some grace. Sometimes, I would be my own worst enemy. I was unkind to myself. My confidence was non-existent. I was that diamond in the rough that Jonathan found one day! But God! Through time and with patience, I developed into a better version of myself. There was more to me that I had no idea about. It was through trauma, loss, ups and downs that I realized I had always been right where I was supposed to be. It is not meant for everyone to understand your journey or the decisions that you made. Your life experiences mold you into what you are intended to be. Most of the steps that I have taken in my life were 80% me doing my own thing.

But that mighty 20%, that was all God! It is amazing how much of a difference 20% makes! That is why people always ask for their 10% military discount! Just imagine if they could get 20%! God has always had His hands on me, even when I detoured from the plan.

As I take you from my high school days to my life in the Army, I want you to know that all things are possible. If you do not get anything else, understand that whatever you are going through is not always meant to last. You will not do everything right. You will make mistakes. Do not take mistakes lightly. Learn your lessons, apply those lessons, teach the next generation, and keep living. My dad always told me, "No matter what, always let your light shine."

Preface

Behind the Scenes

I was born and raised in Jackson, Mississippi, on June 23, 1982. My parents, James and Mimmie Harvey, had been married ten years before they were blessed with me, and then three years later, they were blessed with my brother, Westley "Bugg" Harvey. My dad also had older children, whom I met when I was young but did not get to know until I was almost in middle school. My oldest brother, James Jr., came around more than my other siblings, so everyone knew who he was. He and his family live in Louisiana now. My mom told me about my oldest sister, Yolanda, whenever I saw her pictures in the photo album. She and her family live in Texas now.

James Jr. and Yolanda grew up in Yazoo City, Mississippi, where my dad was from. And from what I remember, my brother Alfred "Peanut" came around more when I was in middle and high school. Peanut grew up in Jackson and went to Lanier High School. He and his family live in Mississippi. I remember meeting my sister Inetta when I was in high school. Inetta also grew up in Jackson and went to Lanier High School. She and her family live in Mississippi. My brother Mario and I were both in the Army. But he came around more as I got older. Mario grew up in Jackson, Mississippi, in the Shady Oaks area. We stayed in touch more than my other siblings, and I did as we got older. He and his family just moved back to Mississippi. I met my late sister Tanisha once, but I don't really remember her, only through a picture. My late brother, James Earl, lived in Yazoo City, and I met him and his family when I was in high school. He was fun to be around, and he and his nephew dusted me and my crew off in basketball during a cookout on the 4th of July.

In my adult life, I realized that once I was old enough to have my own phone and driver's license, I should have also been reaching out to my older brothers and sisters, just as they could've also reached out to me. But I understand that people live their own lives and are focused on caring for their immediate family. I understood that all too well.

It was not until April 2021, when my dad passed away that I realized how much my siblings meant to me. I was always really into my dad's side of the family, but I did not get to see them that much as a child. I got to see my mom's side of the family often during holidays and summer breaks. My family lived in north Jackson, so I did not spend much time with my cousins unless I saw them at church, a holiday dinner, or until I could drive and as I got older. It almost seems as if my parents isolated Bugg and me, but I cannot say if it was intentional. Like all parents, I think they just wanted the best for us.

Looking back, if my parents operated off the mantra of "it takes a village to raise a child," and I had the opportunity to know my entire family, regardless of how it came to be, I believe it would have helped me mentally, physically, and emotionally navigate life. I have a lot of successful people in my family. I have uncles who served in the Army. My grandfather served in WWII. My older brothers are all business owners! My cousins are business owners. I have family members who have multiple degrees and certifications. My family has a history of trailblazing! Understanding what was already inbred in me could have catapulted my confidence and self-esteem. Knowing where you come from sets you on a path to grow into who you should become.

Growing up, I was shy, and I did not really like much attention to be focused on me. Since my parents worked, my brother and I went to almost every daycare in Jackson. You must be from where I'm from to know daycare names like Christian Mission, Mother Goose Academy,

Prep Company, Hanging Moss, Anderson Child Care, and another church I can't remember the name of off Northside Drive. My brother Westley "Bugg" has Down syndrome, and I kept a close eye on him while we were attending each daycare. The problem set was simple. If someone messed with my brother, I fought them. I never cared for kids or people who liked to bully or make fun of people, especially those who could not defend themselves. If you wanted to strike a nerve, that was it for me, especially when the person being picked on was my brother. I have carried this philosophy throughout my life. In essence, I developed a bad temper, and I did not appreciate anyone trying to take advantage mentally or sexually of me or my brother. We had to stick together.

Acknowledgments

I dedicate this work to my loving husband Jonathan, and our beautiful kids, Jya, Ariel, J2, and our grandson Caiden. Be the change that you want to see in the world.

1

Powell Middle School

One of the things I always wanted while growing up was the chance to go to school with my cousins or older siblings. I felt like I needed to be surrounded by people who could help me navigate Middle and High School. I did not care about being popular; I just wanted to be left alone. Because Bugg and I are three years apart, he was just getting to the school when I was leaving the school. After school, we would both ride the van to the daycare we attended at the time. Going to daycare as a seventh grader was embarrassing—no wonder I was getting picked on. Finally, my mother met with one of my best friends at the time, Waynetta's grandmother, and asked if I could ride the bus home with her. That worked out and gave me some freedom until I began high school.

During my 6th-grade year at Powell Middle School, I realized how messy girls can be. Even at daycare, I never really dealt with messy girls. We all played kickball, swapped friendship bracelets, and talked about which boys we thought had a crush on us. I guess that was not enough for the girls in middle school. Some of them were literally sleeping with boys. I had no idea this was going on until one girl came to our school, and her pregnancy began to show. I was shocked. All I knew was to grow up, get married, and then have children. So that caught me totally off guard. One of my good friends, Deven, stayed in North Colony Town homes across from me. She was friends with a girl named Debra. We took a few classes together. I thought I was cool with Debra and all the other girls who talked to me; not most of them did though. One night on the phone, Deven told me to be prepared because Debra told her that she and some other girls were going to jump on me the next day.

I was so confused. I didn't even know I had done anything to Debra or any of the "other" girls Deven had mentioned. I was so mad, and I cried while I was preparing for battle. My mama checked on me for dinner, and she instantly knew something was wrong. I told her what Deven had told me. My mama made a few phone calls, and the rest was history. Jumping on me was never brought up again. Debra even asked me a few days later why I thought she would jump on me. I told her because that's what I was told. I learned my first lesson in dealing with girls who may not like you just because you are you. Wow! That really is a thing. You can literally mind your own business. Or you can sit near or in the sessions when girls are bashing other girls, and you will be the one to take the fall just because of what you allowed yourself to be involved in.

I felt like I was Daniel in the lion's den at Powell Middle School. I did not fit in with the kids there at all. I rocked one ponytail with a bang most of the time, and my hair was not straight but puffy and bright! My hair color matched my hazel eyes. I stuck out like a sore thumb. I did not have the latest fashionable clothes or shoes, but my clothes and I were clean. I knew the answers to questions in class, but I was too embarrassed to raise my hand and bring any attention to myself to answer. Powell Middle School was an entire culture shock and learning experience for me. I learned how to curse, how to eavesdrop, and what bullying meant if you were not one of the cool kids. I also learned how treacherous and messy girls can be. Lastly, I learned how messy boys can be.

When I was at daycare one evening while in the 7th grade, I spoke with a few other girls there, and they explained to me what it means when a girl has her period. My mind was blown. The only time my mama and I spoke about this was when she told me about having hers at the age of 16. Well, I was nowhere near 16, so I assumed, like mother, like daughter, the same thing would happen to me. Ironically, after having this talk at the daycare, I went to school one day, and it was around the 4th period when my stomach started hurting so bad. I twisted and turned in my seat as I tried to complete my work. When I got up to turn my paper in, one of the boys in my class pointed out that I had blood on my shorts. My teacher, Ms. Stewart, pulled me aside and asked me if I knew what was going on. I told her no. She explained it and walked me to the office to call my parents. I was so embarrassed. I don't even remember who came to pick me up, if they brought changing clothes, or if I even went back to class. All I remember is the boy pointing it out and everyone laughing.

The very next day at school, I was so uncomfortable. I felt like everyone was looking at me and talking about me. I did not understand that I needed to change the pad often, especially with a heavy flow. I went from 1st period to 4th period with the same pad on. When I got to 5th period, one boy walked by my desk and said, "Something stinks." Then another boy walked by my desk and said, "It smells like catfish up in here." After that, I determined that it was probably me. I did not know what I was supposed to smell like or how often to change the darn pad.

When I talked to my mama, she asked me why I didn't use the powder and wipes she had given me. I told her my bathroom break was short, and I was too embarrassed to walk out of the stall and throw away all the items. It took me so long to change the pad that I was late for my next class when I finally changed it. My mama looked at me and told me the most reassuring words I needed to hear when she picked me up from daycare that evening. She said, "Mia, every girl or woman goes through this until they hit menopause." I didn't know what menopause was at that time, but it gave me a sigh of relief to know that I was not the only one this craziness happens to. With this incident, I learned that there will be moments in life that you can and cannot control. No matter what the outcome is, you must continue. However, my way of continuing back then was by hiding even more in the shadows and silencing myself not to draw any more attention to myself.

By the time I was in 8th grade, I had seen my first playboy magazine snippet in the gym; I was amazed! I learned how to masturbate. I couldn't tell anyone about that. I learned how to write poetry. I discovered that I was an alto and had a decent singing voice. But the thing I realized that I was really good at and enjoyed as an escape from reality was playing my violin. Ok, let's backtrack a little. I began playing my violin in 6th grade. I was too late to sign up for the band, so Orchestra was left, and I did not have to stay after school to be in it. That was a win for me, daycare, and my parents.

My first teacher was an Asian man named Mr. You. Mr. You was so nice, and he was a good teacher. But we gave Mr. You hell. This is where Waynetta and I became friends. At first, I was getting into it the with a girl named Kenyatta in the class, and then Waynetta got involved. I believe we got into a fight somehow, but we eventually became friends! The common enemy now was Mr. You. We did not listen to him. We came to class late. We climbed the fire escape in the auditorium. We beat up on boys when we were late for class. We were doing the most. When Mr. You finally quit, Mr. Clarke became our teacher. He was African American. We were determined that he liked men and were set out to run him off as well. In 7th grade, Mr. Clarke taped thumbtacks to the neck of my violin so that I would be forced to hold my wrist straight. Waynetta told him that my mama would curse him out, and he would lose his job. She was right. I didn't see my mama curse him out because that's the kind of woman she was. It was implied that she handled it just like she'd handled everything else.

When we returned to school in 8th grade, we had a lady named Ms. Perry. She was also an African American with a different mentality from the two men. She was determined to show us how to play the violin and how to compete. This was amazing. Waynetta and I went to All City and met several kids from all over the state. It was so cool. Of course, we got into a little trouble running around there, but it was all worth it. We got to perform in Downtown Jackson in one of the auditoriums. This was my first glimpse of what dedication could do. I liked this feeling. I wanted to get better and continue to learn how to be the best at playing my violin.

One thing I did not talk about at Powell is all of the very detailed instances of me getting bullied, but yes, it happened. From 6th to 8th grade, I walked on eggshells and tried to stay out of the other kids' way. I went through periods of people stealing my work to turn in, making me do their work, threatening to fight me if I didn't do their friend's work, girls lying on me, boys lying on me, and, of course, being the stinky girl. Through all these things, my parents told me to be the bigger person and look the other way. Correction: daddy told me to knock them out if they put their hands on me. Mama told me to tell the teacher, and if it were only words passed, to work on my comebacks. Snitches get stitches, so I never told the teachers. I just endured the abuse, remained depressed, took my frustrations out on other areas of my life, and barely survived Powell Middle School. When we graduated and left for the summer, I felt like I had done three years the hard way. I just knew that high school couldn't be anything like this.

2

The Summer Before High School

The summer before high school, my mama found a new daycare opening up off Floral Drive. It wasn't far from where we lived in North Colony, and she proposed to the owner that I work there in the nursery for the summer, and Bugg could attend at a discounted price. One of the things I left out is that in middle school, I received a diary, and I wrote down every feeling and thought in it. I have no idea what happened to that diary, but if anyone ever read it, I meant everything I said, and all the things I described about being molested and darn near raped are true. Fast forward, in an effort to watch both my brother and me, we both attended this daycare the summer before I started high school. I worked in the nursery with a girl named Nikki and a lady named Ms. Jones. Ms. Jones' three children also went to the daycare, and she was the head of the nursery. Nikki was the owner's niece. She and I were the same age. Initially, She was cool until this boy named Girad started working at the daycare. I think he was the same age we were. He was light-skinned and wore a low haircut. Nikki was crazy about the boy. He was cool, but I didn't like him like that. Nikki would go back and forth playing with him, and they both often disappeared during the day at times. One day, Nikki left me in the nursery alone while Ms. Jones was at lunch with four babies and one special needs child.

When Ms. Jones returned, Nikki still wasn't back. I did not volunteer any information about where Nikki was or how long she'd been gone, but Ms. Jones figured it out. She informed the owner, and then I started getting dirty looks from Nikki. I let her know that I did not say anything to Ms. Jones. She and I were no longer cool after that. Girad started coming around to the nursery to talk to me on days Nikki wasn't there. By the end of the summer, we exchanged phone numbers. I was preparing to start high school at Callaway, and he was going to Provine. I never saw or heard from him again when school started.

One thing about having a summer job that I didn't realize was that I was getting a check. My mama left that part out when she told me I would be working at the daycare. I made $575 that summer! You couldn't tell me that I wasn't rich. Mama told me that hard work pays off, and I saw this in real time. We went to get school supplies and clothes. I also paid someone to do my hair! High school was going to be a new beginning for me. For the first time ever, I was confident, had money, and had friends going into the 9th grade. I was ready!

3

Callaway High School

My freshman year of high school was a new beginning. In the mornings, I would walk to school and then meet a few friends in the cafeteria for breakfast. Everything was going well until one day in gym class, one of the upper-class girls asked me for some of my candy. For the record, I always had candy or snacks on me. It used to be my side hustle to sell candy and have something others may want to keep them from picking on me. I played basketball with a few other girls in the gym class until we took a break, and I went for my candy. This upperclass girl didn't really ask me; she mainly told me to give her some candy. I instantly went back into my shell from Powell Middle School when kids would bully me. One of the girls I was playing basketball with, named Kim, must've seen the look on my face, and my entire demeanor had changed. Before I could even attempt to tell the girl no, Kim said "No, she's not giving any candy away." The girl looked at her and said something smart, then walked off with her friends. I looked at Kim and thanked her. From that day forward, Kim and I were thick as thieves. Kim was tall, light-skinned, and grew up fighting. She knew how to dress, and she was good at basketball. Kim didn't have a problem telling people about themselves. She was confident, and no one bothered her. By watching Kim in action, I began to learn how to stand up for myself. It did not come easy, and little did I know it would take me well over into adulthood to figure it out.

I also met another friend named Rebecca. We both had a lot in common. We were both shy. Both of our father's names were James. Our moms worked at Bell South, and we were the middle children. I had several classes with Rebecca. She thought I was weird at first, but we soon realized we had much in common. Neither of our parents would spend a lot of money on clothes, shoes, or hair and nails. So, we did what we could with what we had. Rebecca was a comedian. She always had the best jokes, and she was very talented. Rebecca could draw anything. She was also good at coloring and painting her art. One of the other things I admired about Rebecca was that she had unique handwriting. She held her pen and pencil a certain way. Her letters were curved a certain way. Overall, her writing was neat and mysterious. I learned how to sustain good grades, order shoes from magazines, and speak my mind. Rebecca didn't really care about being popular, and she didn't mind telling the popular kids how she felt.

I mentioned Waynetta earlier because we met in middle school. During my 10th grade year, my family moved from North Colony to Robinhood Road. I pleaded with my mom not to send me back to daycare, so she devised a plan with Waynetta's grandma. My mom would drop me off at her house in the mornings, we'd walk to school, and then walk back to Waynetta's house after school. Besides walking to school from North Colony, this was the most freedom I had from 9th to 10th grade. Later on, my parents taught me how to drive, and I got my permit and then my license. My mom gave me her Buick Skylark, and it was on! Then I began to drive Kim, Waynetta, Rebecca, and me to school. Waynetta was quiet but mean. She was hilarious, smart, and had a smart mouth. She was the only person I knew besides my Aunt Lilia who could read a book from cover to cover in less than a day. It didn't matter how long the book was; Waynetta would complete it. Waynetta taught me not to care about what other people think. She sure didn't. If you don't want to hear or know the truth, don't ask her. She didn't hold anything back.

Coriell has been my lifelong childhood friend. We met in kindergarten and literally moved from school to school together from North Jackson to Watkins and back to North Jackson. We lived in Valley North, not too far from each other during my elementary years, but then we moved. Coriell went to Chastain for middle school instead of Powell. Then we met back up at Callaway for high school. Coriell was always like my annoying little brother, but he was older than me. He would get in trouble in every grade we were in. Finally, he'd found something he enjoyed that held his attention in middle and high school, and of course, it was the band. Being in the band changed Coriell's trajectory. His parents were also very supportive and ensured that he and his siblings had all the tools to succeed. Coriell had his car before me and Rebecca. He had a candy apple red Cadillac. Coriell was always very positive, no matter how bad things would seem. He had his band crew, his Valley North crew, and us on the side. Coriell and Waynetta always bumped heads, but we all got along well for the most part. Coriell taught me to always have faith in God and to be positive, and that Tupac was the best rapper alive. Of course, we'd argue years later about the best basketball players, rappers, and career paths.

One thing for sure: this was my crew of friends. We were loyal, and we navigated Callaway High School together. Looking back, we were probably considered misfits early on, but once a few of us joined the Junior Reserve Officer's Training Corps (JROTC), there was no turning back. Curiously, I joined JROTC because I wanted to march in the parades. Coriell would tell us about the parades and how much fun being in the band was. Then I discovered I could also be in the parade by joining JROTC. I had no idea what JROTC was nor what opportunities it would afford me. During my freshman year, I took the class and didn't receive a uniform until time for the Martin Luther King Jr. parade. However, I continued to practice with the JROTC Drill Team and Adventure Training Unit to learn all I could about being a cadet and how to be a good citizen. I really enjoyed learning how to march, do facing movements, and how to compete in competitions.

First Sergeant Webber, Sergeant First Class Lowe, and Sergeant Anderson were my JROTC instructors. Major Bilbrew was the Senior Army Instructor. I took his class my senior year. This group of retired Army leaders set me on my path of interest in the military. They saw something in me that I didn't see in myself. They were encouraging yet blunt and honest. They told me the truth about things and called me out when I tried to hide in the back. I believe it was my sophomore year when all of Jackson Public Schools met at the coliseum for its annual Pass and Review. I moved up to Company Commander and was set out to call commands and march my company during the Pass and Review. Once we arrived and I had seen all the other schools, I felt dizzy and overwhelmed as I stood in front of my company while everyone else got into formation. That morning, I had taken a Benadryl before we left the school, but I didn't eat anything. It was in that moment I stood in front of my company that I almost fell out and got completely nauseous. A few people took me to the back of the formation, and that's when several whispers started. Thankfully, I was able to drink some water, regroup, and get back in front of the formation to march my company through Pass and Review when it was time. This was the first time I was out front, and I froze. My anxiety (which I had no idea that's what it was at the time) had gotten the best of me.

On a side note, my sophomore year was the first time in my life that I had a boyfriend that cheated on me. Not once, but he cheated twice! Let's refer to him as Cheater. Annnnnnd, I took him back. The first time he cheated on me was with a very good friend of mine who was also in JROTC. They never mentioned it to me. I found out about it because a guy in my computer class told me. He only told me because he liked me

11

and didn't want me to be with Cheater. When I asked Cheater, he lied. When I asked my friend, she told me the truth! I was shocked but also appreciated her telling me the truth. We are still friends to this day. Of course, Cheater was forced to come clean, and then I took him back. The next time he cheated, it was with his ex-girlfriend, who had transferred to our school from another school. They both lived in Presidential Hills and rode the same bus, etc. This time, I only found out through what had started as rumors from people who had run in similar circles. Then one of Cheater's brothers told me. But Cheater said it was because they didn't want to see us together. Whatever that means. When I confronted Cheater about it, he said it wasn't true.

Then, one day, as I was walking down the hall at school, and I saw him kissing his ex. Well, that was the benediction. I moved on. I, unlike the other girls he'd slept with, was still a virgin. I was saving myself for marriage. I literally told every guy that wanted to date me the same thing. Some thought I could be swayed, and they eventually gave up. However, Cheater tried to play all angles. All these emotions were going through my mind at the Pass and Review because half of the people who knew us both were in JROTC. They knew we had broken up. They knew why we had broken up. Cheater also started claiming his ex as his new girlfriend. I felt stupid, silly, insecure, and not good enough. Here I was, with all my emotions standing out in front of my company, getting ready to lead a group of people. But how could I? Are they going to listen to me? Will they take me seriously after all the drama? At every turn, I doubted myself, and in an instant, a voice told me to snap out of it. I pulled myself together, and I led my company.

The summer of my sophomore year, I signed up to go to summer camp at Camp Shelby. It was located about an hour and a half away from Jackson. All Jackson Public Schools and schools from other places in Mississippi came to Camp Shelby for summer camp. It was a huge event that I had never heard of. We were split up into different companies and mixed in with other schools when we arrived. I got to know several people from other schools. We had a lot of team-building experiences, like the Leader Reaction Course (with water) and the repel tower. One of the events that I really stood out in was the mock pt test. I won the most push-ups and sit-ups for females overall. I put Callaway High School on the map. After that, most of the other Senior Army Instructors and cadets knew who I was when I went to other drill competitions to compete. SFC Lowe would run us around the quad at Callaway and ensure that we could do push-ups and sit-ups, and run during our Adventure Training Unit weekends.

When SFC Lowe left, both 1SG Webber and MAJ Bilbrew continued to make us do physical fitness. I was never a fast runner, but I could run distance with no problem. When I was announced as the 1st place winner in both categories, the people in my summer camp company went crazy. They cheered me on along with our motto. Inside, I was beaming! I was so proud of myself. It was the first time I saw my hard work pay off. I began to believe in myself more. I began to see that I was not only good at playing my violin but that I also had other talents.

Throughout high school, I worked as a referee at the YMCA. Rebecca shared the information about that opportunity with me. We got paid $10 an hour and worked only three days a week. We refereed Baseball and Soccer for 3–4-year-olds. By the time I was a junior, Kim shared the opportunity with me to work at McDade's, a local grocery store off Northside Drive. It paid $5.15 an hour, but you got more hours throughout the week, plus overtime during holidays. I was never good at math; however, I convinced my parents to let me apply, and I got the job to be one of their cashiers. I showed up to my interview in my JROTC uniform because I had come directly from school.

Mr. McDade was impressed with my uniform and dedication to the JROTC program. We even discussed days I could work and how to request leave during competition days. I was so excited to start! Kim and I worked similar shifts sometimes. We also met a few people who went to Murrah who also worked at the store. Coriell soon got hired as a stocker. Both Callaway and Murrah had taken over McDade's in the evening times. I enjoyed working there. I naturally took pride in being a cashier. With any task, I always wanted to do and be the best at it. Nothing about me was mediocre, nor did I want to be put on the spot for not doing something right. My shyness still wanted to be hidden, but my talent put me on the main stage. I needed to get ready!

My junior year was packed with responsibility. I had to ensure that I managed my time accordingly. I was still a cashier at McDade's in the orchestra, on the JROTC Rifle Team, JROTC Adventure Training Unit, Color Guard Captain, and the Captain of the JROTC Drill Team. My top priority for the Orchestra was to practice and prepare for All-City. In JROTC, it was constant practice for upcoming competitions and football games. I learned to manage my time well. One would think that with all my extra-curricular activities, my grades would be horrible; however, my grades were high Bs and a C+ in math.

The money I made from McDade's, I put gas in my car, kept a few snacks, and put money in my checking and savings accounts at Trustmark weekly. I also kept my hair done. Sometimes I would get my nails done, but mainly for military balls. Playing in the orchestra did not require me to have long nails, so I went most of the time without them. I felt a sense of purpose by being so busy and by making my own money. My mom was probably super happy not to have to always give me money for school. Sometimes, she would still find a way to slip me $5 here or there. Five dollars was a lot back then. I competed for First Chair at All-City and didn't get it, but I played Third Chair anyway. After All-City was the military ball. I ran for Miss LET III. I won! In fact, Major Bilbrew told me that I was two votes away from winning Miss JROTC, but they preferred it to be a senior. I was impressed. I had no idea that people knew me like that. People from the entire Callaway JROTC program voted on the candidates on the ballots. So, it was impressive to me to be a runner-up for Miss JROTC. I took a moment to celebrate my Miss LET III win. It was a goal I had set, and I conquered it. I felt like I was born to compete.

I didn't really care to go, but I went to my junior prom with my friends. The prom was sometime after the military ball, and to me, the military ball was more inclusive, fun, and exciting, and it was with people I liked being around. I didn't really have a lot in common with my other classmates other than being in class with them. So, Waynetta, Shundra, Rebecca, Coriell and I went together when it was time for my junior prom. I can't remember who drove, but we had a blast. We laughed and danced a little. At the military ball, we danced all night. At the prom, we waited for the announcements to be made on who won what. We also took pictures since we looked good, as always. People started fading away as soon as the prom king and queen were named. So, of course, we did too. I don't remember where we ate afterward, but we vowed to have a better time for our senior prom.

4

Why Join the Army?

Going into my senior year of high school, I had taken the ACT twice to compete for a scholarship to go to college. On my first attempt, I scored a 14 and a 16 on my second attempt. Math was not my strong suit, and I was not a good test taker. Needless to say, I was not getting a scholarship. After taking the ACT twice, I applied to Mississippi State, Florida A&M, Tougaloo, Jackson State University, and The University of Southern Mississippi. The truth is, I was not sure what I wanted to go to college to study. All my life, I was told I had to go to college. It was never explained to me how to secure funding to go to college. I had no idea what to major in, how to choose the right college, how to complete FAFSA correctly, and how to negotiate the sticker price at a college. My parents worked, but together, they did not make enough to fund my education. On top of all the talks about going to college, my friends had similar talks with their parents or guardians. Rebecca and Waynetta received academic scholarships for Jackson State University. Coriell received a band scholarship from Jackson State University. I felt like the room began to close in on me as my senior year began to take off, and I still had not locked in the college I wanted to attend, received acceptance letters, or secured funding to attend.

I continued to perfect my craft as a violinist to keep busy and not stress too much about going to college. I competed for First Chair at All-City and won. My teacher, Ms. Perry, introduced me to Dr. Branch, Program Director of the Orchestra at Jackson State University. I auditioned for him in the spring of my senior year, and he offered me a scholarship. I did not provide him an answer right away because I knew it was a big step, and I had to make sure that it was what I wanted to do. I was a good violinist, but it was not my passion. I also got tired of walking around Callaway with my violin and receiving jokes here and there from people. The last thing I wanted was to have the same thing happen to me again in college. I was not having it. I turned down the scholarship.

In JROTC, I held several different titles. Our Drill Team began to place in various competitions. I enjoyed teaching and developing the underclassmen. I had already chosen an underclassman that I began to train without her knowing to take my place after I graduated. I was always forward-thinking. I always cared about what would happen to the people I was leaving behind. 1SG Webber agreed with my successor. She was shy at first but soaked everything up like a sponge. She was very dependable. She had a good sense of humor. When in charge, she took charge. No questions asked. She reminded me of me.

The year went by fast. In the spring, I received a few acceptance letters, but the tuition deterred me from locking in on one college. When I spoke to MAJ Bilbrew, I told him I was considering joining the Marines. He told me I was crazy! He told me to talk to an Army recruiter instead. After all, I was about to complete four years of Army JROTC and receive credit that counted towards obtaining rank as a Private First Class in the Army starting out. I am extremely hard-headed and stubborn. Sometimes it took me a while to make decisions because I was shell-shocked of what could/would/should/might happen. My mother always cautioned me to think about the consequences before deciding. This practice stayed with me well into my thirties. I never wanted to fail. I was not afraid of failing, but I also knew that whatever I decided to do, I would give it my all.

I had the opportunity to go to a National Guard Battle Assembly one weekend. I did not understand what they were supposed to be doing, nor did they stay at the unit long. A few weeks afterward, I contacted a Marine recruiter because I liked their uniform and motto, "The Few, The Proud." The Marine recruiter called me instantly, came to my house, met my parents, and then took me to the station to take the ASVAB. Unfortunately, I scored too low to obtain a job that he thought I deserved. The recruiter continued to entertain me possibly joining the Marines, but I would have to take the ASVAB again when the time came. At this point, I was getting ready for my final Military Ball and Senior Prom. I put everything dealing with the service on the back burner. I temporarily shifted my focus to the 'now' instead of the 'future.' I ran for Miss JROTC and won. I enjoyed my Senior Prom. I competed in the Beauty and Beau Pageant. I did not win, but it was a testament to me coming out of my shell and beginning to gain another ounce of confidence.

Graduation was around the corner. My friends were locked in for Jackson State University. My mom was trying to push me toward Tougaloo, but I was leaning toward attending college out of state. I wanted to go off and see the world. I always wanted to travel. That is another reason the military sounded like a good idea. Back then, there were several commercials about the Army. "Be All That You Can Be!" I graduated with honors from Callaway High School in May 2000. I was still working at McDade's grocery store, and I had yet to figure out funding for college. Because my parents did not want me to go far, I also chose to accept to go to Jackson State University. The difference from my friends is that I did not have a scholarship. A few weeks after graduating high school, I decided to reach out to an Army recruiter. SFC Hunter answered my call. He met with me immediately. I was able to retake my ASVAB. This time, I had studied and taken the practical exercise a few times. The issue was that I still had a super low score. I was not good at testing, no matter what the test looked like. Taking tests always gave me anxiety, and I never slept well or ate well before the assessments.

SFC Hunter showed me jobs that I qualified for with my score. Not knowing what I was getting into, I chose a job that had a $5,000 signing bonus. That was a lot of money for a kid who just graduated high school and still worked for $5.15 an hour. I asked SFC Hunter what the job was. He explained that it was a Petroleum Supply Specialist (77Foxtrot). This Military Occupational Skill (MOS) conducted fuel recirculation and hot and cold refueling of helicopters/planes, as well as dealing with storage, distribution, and accountability of fuel. He had me at $5,000 to sign up to be a fueler. I told MAJ Bilbrew, and he fussed at me about going into the Army Reserves. He told me that I should go on Active Duty instead. My recruiter, SFC Hunter, told me that Active Duty goes to war first. He also told me that being in the Army Reserves, I would not be pulled out of school for war. When people say, "My recruiter lied to me," that is just one example of what they meant! Because I was not 18, due to my birthday being late in the summer, I had to get permission and signatures from both of my parents to join the Army Reserves. My mom did not want me to go at all, so she told my dad to tell me no. The crazy thing is that her plan backfired. I am a daddy's girl through and through. When I sat down with my dad to explain why I wanted to join the military and how it could help me with college and I'd get to travel, my dad still wasn't having it. I got so emotional that I began to cry. I hardly ever cried. The times I did cry were extremely hurtful times for me. Therefore, my dad knew that joining the military meant a lot to me. He gave his blessing, and the rest was history!

5

Basic Training

My time at the Jackson MEPs went fast. I passed my pregnancy test, of course (I was still a virgin)! I did my duck walk to determine the status of my feet and spine. I signed several papers. The last thing was being sworn in. On June 30, 2000, I raised my right hand and repeated after the officer who led me and several others in the oath that would govern my entire career. What a day! My basic training dates were scheduled for mid-July at Fort Leonard Wood, Missouri. I was supposed to go for ten weeks of basic training and ten weeks of Advanced Individual Training at Fort Gregg-Adams (former Fort Lee) after basic. My recruiter set me up to conduct my training without any breaks other than scheduled Christmas leave. My recruiter ensured I knew where to be and when to get on the plane (my first time) from Jackson, Mississippi, to Fort Leonard Wood, Missouri.

My first plane ride was exciting, and I got very nauseous at the same time. I wore a button-down collar shirt and navy-blue jeans. I had one large suitcase with wheels. Once I arrived in Missouri, a reception station of people in uniform got my attention and directed me to a station to get my driver's license checked and to see a copy of a piece of paper I traveled with. Then I was placed in an area with a group of people in civilian clothes. After an hour, we rode a bus to what seemed like the middle of nowhere. We arrived at Fort Leonard Wood. In fact, when we got off the bus, a man with a funny-shaped hat yelled at us and said, "Welcome to Fort Lost in the Woods." I was so confused. The hat looked like something from Yogi Bear. I later found out that the man with the funny-shaped hat was our Drill Sergeant for the Hold Over Detachment. I was assigned to a company and shown my bunk and wall locker area.

Because I had not yet entered basic training, I still had access to my cell phone and my entire suitcase. It seemed I was given so many shots in a single day. Living in an open bay with other females I didn't know was a culture shock. I was a little shy, but when I met another Mississippi girl and a girl from Alabama and Texas, we all stuck together. During holdover, we were tested on the Soldier's Creed and Warrior Ethos, fitted for certain uniforms, given time to work out, and a lot of time to call home. Being in this environment did not seem to be bad at all. However, some people took the hold over time hard. Some people had suicide ideations, and some tried to run away or go AWOL. I was happy to be somewhere new, so I was fine waiting to go to basic training.

It was mid-August, and I was still in the same holdover company. We were told that we had to wait for a company to graduate basic training before we would be shipped to the training area. No one understood what this timeline looked like. Therefore, I knew I would not return to Mississippi in time to start college with my friends. So, I took the time to focus on what I needed to know to be successful when I finally made it over to basic training.

The night it was time to leave and go to basic training, I was split up from my friends that I had bonded with in holdover. I was instructed to grab my bag and get on this tin truck that looked like something you would haul cows in and instructed to put my head in my chest. We later referred to the carts as cattle trucks. I did not notice at the time, but a drill sergeant got onto the cattle truck with us. It was quiet the entire ride over. No one made a sound. You couldn't even hear the next person breathing. Nothing. Silence. Still quiet. It was dark when we left hold over. It was now broad daylight when the brakes of the cattle truck screeched to a halt. The doors of the cattle truck swung open, and the yelling and screaming began! "GET YOUR SORRY ASSES OFF NOW AND TAKE YOUR BAGS OVER THERE! MOVE! MOVE! MOVE! WHAT THE HELL ARE YOU LOOKING AT? DON'T LOOK AT ME! GRAB YOUR SHIT AND GET OVER THERE IN LINE. HURRY UP!" My bag had wheels on it. I tried to roll it as terrified as I was, and I was stopped immediately and told to pick it up and go. Tears rolled down my face as I struggled to carry my bag over to get in line. Everyone was running. There were several drill sergeants everywhere. They were all yelling. It sounded like a bunch of sports announcers yelling at you about a play that was not your fault at the same time. I was in total shock!

Once in line with my bag, I was told to face right and follow the person before me. The person in front of me took off running, and so did I. We all ran down the sidewalk, around this long building, down another long sidewalk, and then back to stand behind our bags. During the run, we were sprayed by someone holding a water hose. This was Missouri in August, so maybe the heat category had something to do with this tactic, but it caught me totally off guard. I honestly thought that I had made the biggest mistake of my life. When I made it back to my bag, I saw a drill sergeant working down the row, emptying each bag. He was roughly and swiftly going through each person's bag and throwing their items everywhere like he was looking for something. When he got to me, he held up the cute underwear that I packed and asked me where the hell was I was going, and he then threw them in the grass. I was so embarrassed.

After he finished tearing up everyone's bags, he told us to face right again and follow the person in front of us. The same thing happened again, and we ran down the sidewalk, got sprayed, ran around the building, got sprayed again, and then made it back to our bags. This time we were instructed to put our bags up, turn right, and follow the person in front of us. Our bags were being stored in the basement area of the building we were running around. Cell phones were taken and placed in lock boxes to which only the drill sergeants had keys. We marched to another building and drew our linen for our bunks. We marched back to secure our linen. Then we were marched to chow. We had to stand at parade rest, come to the position of attention, move forward, and then go back to parade rest until we reached the line and retrieved a tray. The person taking the headcount would tell you to sound off with your last four as the line moved. I never got my food so fast and ate so fast. An entire company's worth of people moved through the chow line in a matter of minutes. It was crazy! I didn't taste my food at all. This was nothing like being in holdover. It was like night and day!

After chow, those of us who did not have all the supplies we needed were marched over to the Post Exchange (PX). We were also allowed one minute, and I mean one minute, to call home to say that we had made it. When it was my turn, I dialed my parent's home number. My mama answered the phone. I told her I made it. She told me she was glad I made it. At that moment, tears fell down my cheeks. Before I could respond with anything else, the Drill Sergeant hung up the phone, and I had to get back in formation. I was devastated. There are several things that I could talk about from my basic training experience, but the ones that changed how I view life are worth mentioning.

My Battle Buddy

My battle buddy, Private Garnica from Guatemala, and I did not get along initially. I could not understand what she was saying, and I guess she could not understand what I was saying because of my accent. We were paired up to go everywhere with each other, and we were bunkmates. She was very unorganized but could make the sharpest edges on her bed with her sheets and green wool blanket. My edges needed a lot of work. Randomly, drill sergeants came into our bay, flipped bunks, and poured out wall lockers if they were not secure. Every day, it was a scene. One day, my bunk got flipped because my edges were not perfect triangles. Private Garnica did not help me out. She just looked and spoke in her native tongue with someone else while I struggled to get my mattress down. A few other girls helped me get my mattress off the wall locker and put it back on the top bunk. Private Garnica just watched.

One day, we returned from church, and the drill sergeants had struck again. It was their tradition to trash a wall locker if it was left unsecured. Well, guess who left their wall locker unsecured? Yep, it was Private Garnica. The drill sergeants had poured all her shampoo onto her physical fitness uniform, trashed all her feminine items, dumped everything out of her small dresser onto the floor, and tore up all her envelopes and stamps. They pushed her entire wall locker over into the wall. It was like a leaning tower when we got there. Private Garnica instantly started crying and she was embarrassed and hurt. I almost did not help her. She never tried to help me. Without saying anything to her, a few other girls and I just started helping her pick everything up, relocated the wall locker, rinsed the shampoo out of her uniforms, and once it was all done, I gave her a few of my envelopes and some of my stamps. Writing letters home was the main way to communicate with the outside world back then. That day changed our relationship. Private Garnica taught me how to fold my edges properly to make that crisp triangle. I showed her how to organize and lay out her wall locker. We also checked behind each other to make sure our stuff was secure. From that day on, we got in trouble together, we ate together, and most of all, we learned about each other's homes. When we graduated from C-2-10, we went to different places. Our paths never crossed in the Army again. I learned that no matter how things may seem when you first meet someone new, you should give it time and give them a chance. Do not be so quick to judge someone. That person may have something to offer to make you a better person and likewise.

The Gas Chamber

I can honestly say that you will be successful if you listen to what your drill sergeant is teaching and training you on; remember it, practice it, and apply it. Before going to the gas chamber, I went through the training and several classes. I paid attention and followed all the steps to be able to put my mask on before nine seconds was up. The entire time, the drill sergeant told us it was a matter of life and death. Being able to put my mask on in time meant the difference of my family ever seeing me again or not. I took this training very seriously. The day that we were scheduled to go to the gas chamber, my drill sergeant told our platoon to eat whatever we wanted at lunch chow. I should have known at the time that this was a setup. He told us that we could have ice cream and cake and to drink plenty of milk. I had cake and plenty of milk. When we left chow, we marched until we saw the cattle trucks. Once piled in, we were off to the gas chamber. Upon arrival at the chamber, there were three stations we had to go through before going into the chamber. Once the stations were done, we were instructed to line up in six rows.

When it was my row's turn to enter the chamber, we all had our masks on. We ran around once and stood in a line facing the person in the middle who gave us our next instructions inside the chamber. We had to break the seal (lift our masks off), take a breath, put it back on, and secure it. When I lifted my mask off and took a breath, I puked instantly. Because the gas was so strong, I hurried and put my mask back on and continued to puke in my mask with it on. The next thing we were told was to take our masks all the way off, and we could not leave until everyone did. I had already puked everywhere and in my mask, so I took it off. The space we were in suddenly began to get smaller and smaller. I could not

25

breathe. The gas choked me. I just wanted out, but we were instructed not to run out, or we would have to come back. Once the door opened, I said my last four and stumbled out of the chamber. We had to keep walking straight into the open field, flap our arms, and take deep breaths. We were told not to rub our eyes or our skin. Of course, some people did, and their eyes had to be flushed out with water. I had no idea that I was claustrophobic until this day. After this experience, I never wanted to be anywhere tight, closed in, small, or restrictive. The good news is that I proved to myself that I could break the seal and reseal my mask with no problem. Even with puke inside, my mask worked. The bad news is that I immediately panicked whenever I saw white smoke during ranges or field training exercises, thinking it was gas and that I needed to put on my mask.

Basic Rifle Marksmanship (BRM)

The most challenging training for me was Basic Rifle Marksmanship (BRM). In JROTC, I learned how to shoot a rifle that was more like a pellet gun. I shot at paper targets indoors. The pellet gun did not have a lot of kickback. Although we worked on breathing in JROTC, it did not prepare me for BRM at basic training. There were so many things to learn about how to fire my M16 properly. The barrel was long, and I learned to engage my target using the iron sites on my M16. Firing was only one part of learning about this weapon. How to breathe. How to aim. How to squeeze the trigger. How to assemble and disassemble the weapon. How to clean the weapon. How to store the weapon. How to carry the weapon safely. Learning about the recoil of the weapon was the first time my drill sergeant caught me off guard. We were all side by side in the grass after completing the "dime-washer drill" when my drill sergeant walked down the line, kicking the barrel of everyone's weapons, that did not have their cheek to the buttstock and nose to the charging handle. He said we also needed to know what the recoil felt like.

When he kicked my weapon, my M16 hit my nose so hard I had a bruise. One person's nose got broken in our platoon. Now I understood what he said to do, but I did not understand why we had to do this, until it took me forever to zero my weapon by the time we went to the range. It was hot one day and cold the next day during BRM. The principle of cheek to buttstock and nose to charging handle was so that I could have the same sight picture when aiming at my target. During my remedial training, I wondered why he did not just say that! I was so frustrated. I realized I performed better when I knew "why" I was doing something versus just doing it because you said do it. My remedial training went well, and I was able to zero the next day. It took me four times to hit more than 23 targets in a single go. The first time I attempted to qualify on the pop-up targets, I was aiming way too high. I also had no idea the targets would pop up the way they did. It made me think of playing Duck Hunt on Nintendo, except all the targets were green and popping up out of the ground. With my birth control glasses that the Army prescribed me, I could see everything. I just did not do well in prone unsupported. I was giving them targets hell from my foxhole, though. The days got longer and hotter, and sometimes they got colder and rainier. The entire time was a test of my faith. I had to ask God to help me pass BRM. I did not want to be a recycle and be moved to another basic training company with people I did not know. I wanted to finish basic training with the people I started with. I was determined. I made it and I thanked God in that moment.

Drill Sergeant Williams

I had one female drill sergeant, Drill Sergeant Williams, during the first four weeks of basic training. She was a tall Puertorican lady who looked like she was in her late twenties. I loved everything about Drill Sergeant Williams. She called cadence that motivated me every time we stepped off. She was soulful. She was confident. She would run and call cadence during physical fitness formations to motivate us. She was fast and she took time to motivate those that did not run as fast. She inspired me to want to be just like her. I was determined to be a drill sergeant one day, too. Drill Sergeant Williams did not take any mess from the male drill sergeants, and she was the only female drill sergeant in our entire company. I was so glad that she was in our platoon. I overheard her say once that her ex-husband was a medic who worked somewhere on Fort Leonard Wood. She never wore a wedding ring, so this was interesting to hear. So, you could be a female leader, married or divorced, and still fulfill your obligations to the nation? I didn't realize it at the time, but there was so much that I did not understand about women who served. One thing about Drill Sergeant Williams' voice is that you knew when she was coming, and her leadership presence was always evident.

The Company Commander

The last hard task I had to complete in basic training after my final field training exercise was the longest road march ever! After being in the field, tired, stinky, and feet worn out, we changed our socks and shirts and began marching during the wee hours of the morning. I believe the final road march was ten miles; do not quote me on that. I remember carrying my weapon. I remember having my rucksack. I remember taking frequent tactical halts with my company off of the road and drinking water. I had no idea what mile we were on or how far we had to go, but I remember a small voice walking beside me and asking me how I was doing. I did not want to answer incorrectly, so briefly, I looked over and saw an African American female captain. She was shorter than me but moved very swiftly during the road march. I was instantly inspired and quickly answered, "Yes ma'am, I am ok." She responded with, "Good to hear. Keep it up; you're almost home." At that moment, I knew I wanted to be the leader that inspired others.

I do not remember my Company Commander's name, but I remember her smile. I only saw her two other times during basic training. I saw her at our company picture day and again at our graduation. I would have liked to see our commander more so that I could truly understand what a commander did. When I was a company commander in JROTC, I was always with my company during JROTC labs. I knew the people in my company and encouraged them to get involved with one or two of the after-school activities. In basic training, I was unsure of my company commander's duties. I knew that my Drill Sergeants were always with us, and they were also our disciplinarians. Who was really in charge?

Basic Training Graduation

As my basic training time ended at Fort Leonard Wood, Missouri, I felt a huge sense of accomplishment. I conquered several fears. I learned a lot about myself as a person and as a female entering a male-dominated profession. As I stood in formation, wearing my green pickle Class A uniform with my brown Army birth control glasses, I took a deep breath and released it into the atmosphere. After we marched on and off the field, we had to stay in formation until our parents came to us. My mama walked right by me. I shed a tear. Then, between her and my dad, they realized where I was. They quickly came to me and hugged me. I understand why they did not recognize me. When I left home, I weighed 117 lbs. When I graduated basic training, I weighed in at 125 lbs. Not only did I have big glasses, but I also gained some healthy weight. I was able to leave the company area and go to the main px with my family and spend time with them for a few hours before I had to be back at the company area. It was refreshing to break away from such an intense environment, even if it was for a short time. When I returned, I said goodbye to my family as I loaded my bags to prepare to depart to Fort Gregg-Adams (former Fort Lee) for my Advanced Individual Training. I was ready for the next part of my journey.

Advanced Individual Training

Leaving basic training, I was motivated. I was determined to do well at Advanced Individual Training (AIT) so that I could get back home and hopefully enroll in Jackson State University by summer. At the beginning of October, I began taking classes that taught me how to be a Petroleum Supply Specialist. Our platoon was split into two classes. My class had a short little prick that was our class leader. He, of course, got in trouble in November, and the next person in line took his position temporarily. I'm not sure about all the specifics of the temporary replacement, but I was asked to be the next class leader. I happily accepted. My instructor saw something in me that I tried to hide being around new people. As the class leader, I was responsible for taking accountability for my classmates and marching us back and forth from the training area. I enjoyed marching them. It took me back to my JROTC days. I was confident when I marched the class. I was soulful in my cadence calling.

I received compliments from my instructor and other instructors. I also received compliments from a few of my classmates. Other than that, I was quiet. I worked hard to score well on each of my exams. I did well on my hands-on assessment. I did not graduate in the top of my class, but I did graduate. Army training is not hard. Repetition, studying, and applying what you have been taught is the best way to pass any Army training. If you fail, it is because you are not trying or don't care. I always cared about doing well. AIT is where I began to be sure of myself and what I had to offer.

I continued to play it cool during AIT when it came to meeting new people other than the girls who stayed in the same room with me. We were in a four-person room in the barracks. My battle buddies were cool. One of the things I enjoyed in AIT was making extra money when people did not want to pull their fireguard shifts. In basic training, pulling your shift was non-negotiable. In AIT, you could make a fortune back then. The shifts were an hour a piece during the week and two hours a piece during the weekend. The shifts were rotated throughout the entire Victor Company. A few older girls in our platoon never wanted to do their shifts. I charged $50 an hour. So, I always had a little extra money. I was amazed at how people totally disregarded money and the rules. I, on the other hand, did not mind. People started recommending me and my battle buddy Arie to do their shifts. Arie and I were about the same color and build, but she was taller than me. Our Drill Sergeant used to get us mixed up all the time. We were always together, too. She was from Alabama. She was quiet, and when we graduated, she went to Fort Campbell, Kentucky. She was Active Duty, and I was a Reservist.

I knew I was one step closer to home when I saw my battle buddy, Anita Brown, at AIT! We quickly got everyone from Mississippi together to take pictures and get to know each other. The cool thing was that we were all going back to Mississippi after AIT. Anita was ahead of my class, so she left and headed back. One of our other battle buddies, Derrick Sterling, also left and returned home. I would graduate within the next month and head back to 894th Quartermaster Company also. It was motivating to see, and it definitely helped me finish strong. AIT taught me patience. It taught me how to negotiate with people. It showed me how to be more outspoken and confident in my own abilities. Basic training taught me how to be a good person, a good Soldier, and a good battle buddy. AIT taught me how to apply what I learned from basic training and when to deviate. AIT gave me a more thorough glimpse of dealing with people one-on-one.

Better Late Than Never

After graduating high school in May 2000, I joined the Army on June 30, 2000. I spent the rest of the year in Basic Training, began Advanced Individual Training (AIT) in late fall, and completed AIT in March 2001. When I returned to Mississippi, it was too late to enroll in Jackson State University's spring semester. I decided to get a job at Chuck E. Cheese until I could enroll in Jackson State University in the summer. I was very excited to start college. My friends were finishing their freshman year, and here I was beginning. I did not think of it as a loss; I thought of it as better late than never. When choosing majors, I chose between English and History. Both only had one math class. Math was my least favorite subject in school, so I decided to play to my strengths. I chose to be an English Major. It was the best decision I could have made. My classes and the instructors were amazing. I learned so much about trailblazers in Mississippi and at Jackson State University. I had a sense of pride about Jackson State and every opportunity it afforded me.

6

Terrorist Attacks

I was in Dr. Hilliard Lackey's History class on September 11, 2001, when terrorists flew planes into the Twin Towers in New York City. All schools closed early that day. The nation was on high alert as two other terrorist plane attacks happened. Everything happened so fast. I had just jump-started my college career. I was using my G.I. Bill and work-study to pay for college. It took me almost a year to figure out how to pay for college financially, and then a threat to the nation occurred. My Reserve unit called me to alert me later that week. I was potentially going to be leaving on a deployment. I began to prepare to disenroll from college temporarily. I packed all my TA-50 and had several conversations with my parents. I was not worried about deploying. In fact, I was more concerned with missing school than anything.

As you know, nothing in the Army happens fast. The terrorist attack happened in 2001. The military started deploying instantly to Iraq and Afghanistan. My Reserve unit did not mobilize to Fort Campbell, Kentucky, until 2003. As deployment came near, I thought about my recruiter, SFC Hunter, telling me that only Active Duty deploys and that by going to Reserves, I would not have to deploy or be pulled out of school. Boy, did he tell a tall one!

A portion of my Reserve unit first mobilized from Jackson, Mississippi, to Greenwood, Mississippi, to link up with another unit. Once united, a deployment farewell happened, and we were off to Fort Campbell, Kentucky. It all seems like a blur; however, I am not sure what month we made it to Kentucky in 2003, but it seemed like we were one of the only units there. We conducted lanes training and medical lanes. I don't remember taking a pt test, but I believe we did go to the range. I remember that our First Sergeant looked like the man on the KFC Logo, and the Company Commander looked like the Pillsbury Doughboy. The entire unit did not qualify to deploy as a unit. Instead, they asked volunteers to deploy to Afghanistan for six months to work on a Forward Area Refueling Point (FARP). One of my battle buddies, Specialist Crosby, was a 77L (Fuel Tester). She and this other female NCO were required to go. Eight fuelers, 77Fs, were still needed. After formation one day, it was announced again that volunteers were needed. I looked in the back of the formation and saw Sho and Mack. I knew that Sho and Mack did not do hard labor whatsoever. To see them volunteering for the deployment, I was shocked! I thought to myself, if they can do it, I know I can do it. I had already been taken out of college that semester, and I would have to wait before I could get back in for the following spring semester, so I decided to volunteer. I had no idea that my life after this deployment would never be the same.

7

Deployment Life

I hit the ground in Afghanistan, and it was like something from the movies. I was so paranoid about Osama Bin Laden unleashing nerve agent poison that I kept my gas mask close by, and I used to sleep with it on my chest. As we trained with a National Guard unit that was already working on Bagram Airfield, I began to learn more about my job as a fueler. AIT was the last time that I had re-circulated fuel from bags. Here I was on a deployment, learning to do so in real time. I liked being a fueler. My favorite parts were both hot and cold refueling. When Black Hawks and Chinooks flew in, they would keep their engines running for hot refueling so they could get out fast. Some Black Hawks turned their engines off. When C130s and C5s landed, they would shut down their engines for a cold refuel. The pilots were cool. They used to bring us random items sometimes. My adrenaline would always amp up when I got a chance to do a hot refuel. The blades are going, the engine is hot, and the pilot signals me to approach the bird. We got so good at FARP operations that sometimes, only two of us would go out at a time. One person would run the pump, and one person would do the refuel.

Now and then, we would get busy, but not too busy. This brings me to the other part of my job while deployed. If I was not working on the flight line, I was in the fuel yard where Pakistan Drivers brought fuel in 5,000-gallon tankers for us to download at our fuel farm (i.e., huge fuel bags). We worked in small crews. One of us would run the pump, and another would check the seals again on the tanker, take the fuel stick, dip the tanker to see how much fuel was delivered, and cross-reference that number with what we actually received on the pump. Needless to say, fuel was always missing! Our team did our best to report real numbers. One of the duties my Battle Crosby had was to go outside the gate and check the seals on the tankers first. The Marines in the Tower were covering her as she walked out. One day, I walked out of the gate with her to see what it was like. It was a little scary but not too bad. The Afghan people were going on about their day as usual. The kids tried to sell anything they could to get money, water, or food from us. We were instructed not to interact with the kids. They could be tricky sometimes. I liked experiencing a different culture and getting a chance to appreciate the little things.

I spent my 21st birthday in Afghanistan. I was not given the day off, but I was given the shit detail. Oh, that's exactly what it was too! My job was to meet up with the two Afghans that drove the porta jon cleaning truck, ride around Bagram to each of the different camps within, and supervise them cleaning each porta jon. I rode in the truck with them as their escort. They, of course, already knew the route. They were shocked that I was a "girl soldier" and the same color as them. I had my M16 Rifle, with live rounds, as I rode in the truck and escorted them for my detail. At lunchtime, they met up with some other Afghans who worked at the camp. We sat in a big open field with concrete bunkers in an L-shape. Inside the concrete bunkers, the Afghans cooked and sat beside each other to eat. The two guys I was escorting wanted me to sit and eat with them. I told them I was on duty. They insisted and also explained to me that it was rude not to. I washed my hands, sat, and ate with them. We had chips (French fries) and halal bread. Whatever cream they used on the bread was delicious. Let me end this with, I didn't see anyone else wash their damn hands! Lol! But I was hungry, and that food they hand-made in a darn concrete barrier was amazing! Yes, my stomach was torn up the next day, but I appreciated the gesture.

When I returned to my tent, I wanted to burn my uniform for that smell. But I didn't have that many uniforms, so I washed it and kept it moving. That day, I learned about another culture. They valued different things. They genuinely cared about the simple things in life. If they were in charge of doing a job, no matter what that job was, they took pride in getting it done. I am also a firm believer in doing the very best at whatever task or job I am doing.

After my unit had fully taken over from the National Guard unit, they re-deployed, and we were officially over FARP operations. The first thing that our NCOIC did was split us up into two 12-hour shifts. Renee and I were on day shift. Everything was going fine until one day; my NCOIC lured me behind a hesco wall that was on the other side of the pump and proceeded to grope me and unzip the flight suit that I was wearing at the time. I was devastated. I pushed him and ran away. I stormed into the connex-like office, grabbed my M16 and book bag, and walked back to my tent on Camp Blackjack as fast as I could. I was dating at the time and told my boyfriend what had happened. I was so scared and felt bad about what happened.

My battle, Renee asked me what had happened. Neither one of us knew what to do after being sexually assaulted by our supervisor. Neither did my boyfriend. He confronted our NCOIC, and they said they had a few words. I did not sleep well that night. I felt dirty. I felt like it was my fault for wearing my flight suit and only a t-shirt, sports bra, and boy shorts underneath. Maybe my appearance enticed my NCOIC. Maybe I am the reason this happened because I was too friendly. I was never interested in that man, nor did I indicate that I was. Then something weird happened. The next day, he sent a message and gave me the day off. While I was off, he brought me a tv. I didn't have a tv. I never said I wanted one, but this was considered a luxury when deployed. When he came to the tent, I froze. I didn't know what to say. He just talked to me, barged in, and set up the TV like nothing had happened. I was so confused. He didn't tell me that I should not say anything, but I felt it was implied that I better not say anything. I didn't know what to do at that point. I later found out that my NCOIC was going around telling other people his version of what happened in case it ever came up again. I knew how popular he was with the First Sergeant and other high-ranking officials; thus, no one would believe me anyway. I regret never speaking up for myself. If he did that to me, there is no telling how many other female Soldiers he has assaulted. I wish I could have that day back so that I could act. That is a life lesson that I would carry with me throughout the rest of my military career.

After being sexually assaulted and not knowing who to talk to or how to handle it, I went a little rogue. I was back and forth with my then-boyfriend. I met another guy from another unit, and we started kicking it, which brought so much friction to me and my unit. Then, one day, one of the guys I considered my big brother pulled me to the side and talked to me. He talked to me about being clear with people about my intentions. By intentions, he really meant with men. I heard him and didn't hear him and ended up looking like a fool. The guy from the other unit left and had a whole family back at home! I had no idea about all that. When he left, of course, I made up with my boyfriend and tried to focus on more positive things that I could do while deployed. I trained and took my Army Physical Fitness Test (APFT). I wanted to compete to be promoted to Sergeant (E5) before leaving Afghanistan.

The run route on Bagram Airbase was one mile up and one mile back. The stretch seemed to be so long, and I had a hard time pacing myself. I never gave up on myself or what I knew I needed to accomplish to move to the next rank. It was a challenge, but I eventually passed it. I could always run distance, but I did not like sprinting. When I learned how to combine the two, I was able to decrease my two-mile run time and pass my APFT for my age group. I still could not get my packet solidified to make Sergeant until I returned home from Afghanistan a few months later.

Going through adversity, ups and downs, trying to figure out how to be in a relationship, learning a new culture, and learning a lot about how people truly are set me on a different path as I was getting ready to pack up and leave Afghanistan. I always talked to Renee about going back to Jackson State University when I got home. I wanted to join ROTC and become an officer. I wanted to be a member of Alpha Kappa Alpha Sorority, Incorporated. I wanted to go on full-time active duty once I completed ROTC. After being deployed in a large country but living in what seemed like a small space I wanted to get away from my hometown and explore and continue to travel the world. So, I set goals and began to take the steps I needed to reach each one. By December of 2003, I had redeployed back to the States. My then ex-boyfriend - now friend - and I met one last time once we returned to our home station. Who knew that my friend would remain connected to me for the rest of my life?

8

Motherhood

I returned to the United States in December of 2003 from Afghanistan. I immediately contacted the JSU Admissions Office to re-enroll for the spring semester. I had a lot of time on my hands in between trying to go back to school and carefully planning my next moves to accomplish my goals. I also reunited with a few of my high school friends and ROTC buddies I met before leaving for deployment. I hit up an old flame or two as well. I wanted people to know that I was back. However, I was not back like the "Mia" I had been before I left. I was a little more ruthless and carefree but ready to get what I wanted out of life. Getting back into school was not hard. Nothing really changed with my family once I returned, or so I thought. I still lived at home with my parents and brother while attending JSU. Did I want to stay on campus? Sometimes. I believe I would've had way more freedom. I would have gotten the complete college experience. But would I have had the same outcomes? Who knows. I was back in ROTC and back to taking classes for my major. Between SFC George, Dr. Chamberlin, Dr. Lackey, and Dr. Ginn, I was always grounded and focused on what I needed to do to graduate and become an officer.

Anyone who truly knows me knows that I love to eat. I have always been greedy when it comes to food, especially something that I like. Tacos started becoming one of my favorites since I tried them while away. One day in January, I ate tacos and got really sick. I didn't think anything about it. Later that week, I ate something else and felt really bad. My mama suggested that I take a pregnancy test. I laughed and said, I will, but I know that is not what's wrong. Maybe I'm still adjusting to being back in the States, or so I thought.

One day, I went to Fred's and got a pregnancy test. It came in a pack of two. I followed the instructions, and I took one with my mama on the other side of the door. It said positive. I never followed directions verbatim, so I figured maybe I did something wrong. So, I took the second pregnancy test. It said positive. Alright, it's time to call a doctor now. My mama helped me set up an appointment to see a doctor. When I went to the doctor, they took a blood sample and tested it. The results came back that I was not pregnant. Then, a few days later, I received another call from the doctor. I went back for another test. I was pregnant. Wow! I was shocked! I have no idea why people are always shocked when they get pregnant when they are out doing all the right things to get pregnant! Lol. But yeah, I was shocked. In a blink of an eye, everything flashed before my eyes.

I called to tell my ex-boyfriend, who had relocated to Chicago, gotten a job and had planned to remain there. I could tell in his voice that he, too, was shocked. My parents were shocked. My daddy didn't say a lot, but my mama did say to me, and I quote, "Mia, I'm not mad at you, but I am very disappointed in you." I carried her words with me throughout my pregnancy until the birth of my beautiful daughter. The truth was that I could have been more responsible. I knew what I wanted to do, and I had a plan to get there. But on September 9, 2004, my world changed. Most people have an 'a ha' moment. The birth of my daughter was my 'a ha' moment. Oh my goodness! I have a little me! She was perfect in every way.

When Ariel was born, she had to have my middle name! After all, she was my mini-me. Ariel Magdalene Harvey instantly inspired me to continue on a path that could lead to success. I knew that I wanted to be the best role model, parent, confidant, voice of reason, motivator, and protector that I could be. I knew I had to be prepared to provide for her no matter what was going on in relationships I either had or no longer had. Because of Ariel, I now had a more defined purpose and obtainable goals. With my parents' support system, I could reach my short-term goals, one goal at a time. I was blessed, and I knew it. Now, it was time to do the work.

9

Leader Development Advance Camp (LDAC)

After having Ariel and recovering physically and mentally, I was able to start running again and training for my Army Physical Fitness Test. At this point, I was actively back in Jackson State's Army ROTC program. I took a year to learn how to swim in order to pass the Commissioning Swim test. The next step was to attend the Leader Development Advance Camp (LDAC) at Fort Lewis, Washington, in the summer of my junior year. How well I performed at this camp would influence what I branched prior to commissioning as a second lieutenant in the United States Army. The camp also determined whether I received an active-duty or Reserve slot.

LDAC was the first time I had to leave Ariel for training for longer than a weekend. She was about five months old. My parents and her Uncle Bugg took care of her while I went to LDAC. SFC George always instilled in us that we had to be better than our competition. Because we were coming from an HBCU, we had to work harder to perform well and obtain what we wanted out of LDAC and the Army. Understanding your weaknesses and strengths gives you the advantage over whomever or whatever you are up against.

I had three weaknesses: sprinting, Night Land Navigation, and fear of water. I had no problem running long distances at a 9-minute mile pace. I did not appreciate having to sprint at a 7-minute mile pace! So I worked on running correctly, breathing correctly, and stretching correctly. I passed my Army Physical Fitness Test (APFT) with no problem. I can contribute that to running through West Jackson in formation during the wee hours of the morning. You never know what you may encounter.

Land navigation was always a challenge. But it was one of the things SFC George harped on the most. He would take us on field training exercises, drop us off to get our pace count, and then give us time to go back. I got lost so many times! My battle and line sister, Montia, was really good at land navigation. She would literally run to some of her points. She helped me realize that I needed to take time to plan my route to get to my points and how to plan backward based on where my farthest points were. Thank God for my battle. To this day, we are still really good sisters and battles. However, at LDAC, I passed day land navigation with no problem, but one of my points for night land navigation was incorrect. It wasn't that I was scared of the dark; it was more of me being scared of snakes. I could see them in the daytime but could not spot them at night with a red lens flashlight. I had to do remedial training for night land navigation. I went back out the next night, and I got all my points. Again, it always goes back to the technique and the mindset. I knew that I had to pass this to successfully pass LDAC.

As for swimming, I passed my test before arriving at LDAC, and it was the only way SFC George let me attend. I had to swim for ten minutes without stopping and tread water for five minutes. However, there were other water events at LDAC that I had no idea I had to partake in. I immediately got nervous and shut down. To test the ability of cadets prior to the combat water survival test, we had to swim from one end of the pool to the halfway point. I froze, and I was classified as "not a strong swimmer." So I went to a different line. Most of us were black as I looked around the line I was referred to. Why can't black people swim?

Because we don't play like that! Lol, I think it also goes back to control. I knew I needed to be in control, but you panic when the water moves you and you have no grip on anything. But seriously, we were all on the side in a separate line as we went through a series of instructions on how to pass the survival test. This was a very humbling experience. It was also one that I believe SFC George tried to prepare us for. He knew the statistics for black cadets, especially those from HBCUs, and the passing rates at LDAC.

I quickly regrouped and focused on the tasks at hand. When it was time for me to jump in the deep end with my LBE and weapon on, ditch the LBE, and swim with my weapon to the other side, I panicked, but I remembered how I passed my swim test in the first place. I was able to swim on my back! So, I used that to my advantage and passed that portion of the test. When it was time for me to jump off the diving board and then over to the side of the pool, I was a nervous wreck. But I remembered that my body naturally wanted to float while treading water for my test, so I used that. I cried to myself as I climbed up the ladder of the diving board. I walked out to the edge and saw the lifeguards waiting at the bottom. I said a quick prayer with my eyes, took a deep breath and stepped off. SPLASH!!!! As soon as my body naturally floated back to the top, I frog-swam over to the side of the pool. Mission complete! What's next?

Peer evaluation during LDAC was also a part of our packets at the end of camp. We were broken down into squads, platoons, and companies. During Situational Training Exercises (STX) lanes, we took turns being evaluated on different Battle Drills, receiving a mission, and briefing the mission using a 5-paragraph Operations Order and a sand table. We were also graded on the rehearsals we conducted prior to the step-off. At the end of the mission, we discussed the actions and then changed out with the next cadet that was called to execute the next mission. STX Lanes training was mostly discussed during our ROTC Labs with the upper classmen and during FTXs. SFC George spent a lot of time with us on understanding how to receive, write, and execute an operations order. I truly despised this at the time! It has been very beneficial to know and understand the order process throughout my military career. At the foundational levels of learning, concepts are born, practiced, and soon can become a mastered skill.

After completing LDAC, I began my senior year at Jackson State. I branched Quartermaster, and I received Active Duty! I must be honest with you. I put my name in the hat for the Medical Service Corps. They did not look my way for that at all. I was happy with Quartermaster because that is what I was when I was an enlisted Soldier. So, if it ain't broke, don't fix it! In the Spring, I pledged and became a member of Alpha Kappa Alpha Sorority, Incorporated, Graduated Cum Laude with a Bachelor of Arts in English, and Commissioned as a 2nd Lieutenant in the United States Army. I rendered my first salute to then SGT Sterling (SFC Retired), and three of my mentors, MAJ (RET) Bilbrew, SFC (RET) Lowe, and 1SG (RET) Webber, were present along with my Dad, Mom, Bugg, and friends.

10

Dog-Faced Soldier

How I ended up at Fort Stewart is a blur, but I definitely wanted to go to a duty station that I thought was close to home. En route to Fort Stewart, I did what Soldiers do; I got married before I made it there. It was common in the Army to meet someone during training, fall in love, and marry them. This, in fact, happened a lot in the Army! For me, it was during my BOLC training at Fort Benning, Georgia. The Gentleman graduated from Virginia Military Institute. I may have been the blackest, black girl he'd ever dated! Lol! Some would say that he was black on the outside and somewhat conflicted on the inside. I thought he was the perfect gentleman. He didn't have any kids. I had my daughter, who was almost two.

When he met my parents, they liked him. Of course, he was different from any guy I'd ever dated up to that point. When he took me to meet his mom and grandmother, his grandmother was sweet. His mom did not want anything to do with me once he told her he wanted to marry me. The bottom line is that I had a child already, and she told him, "She is just a baby mama looking for a baby daddy. She is a gold-digger," and that hurt me so badly. It hurt even more because The Gentleman took it upon himself to tell me that his mother had said that about me. I was even more upset when I realized he did not take up for me. In fact, he never really did when it came to his mom. For the record, he was an officer, but he did not have any money. Lol. Nobody did. Back then, 2nd Lieutenants would ball hard and be stupidly broke. I did not ball hard; I always sent money home to take care of my daughter and her school and to help my parents as needed. His mom and dad were not together. His dad was in the Army and lived somewhere else. His mom still lived at her mom's house. So yeah, we were not going to get along, even if she ever tried to come back and apologize.

The gentleman went to Ranger School, and my daughter and I went to Fort Stewart. Before The Gentleman and I could really begin to know one another, we were mostly apart. A few words were said and both of us had mentally moved on. There was no more to really discuss. I was petty. I gave the Soldiers in my platoon all the stuff he left behind. It took some convincing, but I finally returned his VMI Ring. I never wanted it; I was just being spiteful at the time. The divorce was uncontested, and we both happily moved on. It was six months of my life that I could not get back, but what the future held was much more rewarding.

One of the first things I did at Fort Stewart as a platoon leader was take my platoon to the field. I had only been in the company for about three weeks, and the lady I took over from moved up to be the executive officer of the company. That lady was Randalle Darden, now Lieutenant Colonel Randalle Carter. She and her platoon sergeant moved up to headquarters while my new platoon sergeant, Killa, and I took over our new Distribution Platoon. I had so much personal stuff going on with The VMI Gentleman and trying to get the divorce finalized at the time that I almost broke down when told about the field training exercise. It was just too much. I had to coordinate with my parents or my daughter's dad to meet me halfway to get Ariel and take her back to Mississippi until I returned from the field. I did not have a Family Care Plan set up at the time, nor did I know it existed.

Fort Stewart was about ten hours away from Jackson, MS. Ariel's dad said he would meet me halfway. So, we put the plan in motion. Killa covered for me while I drove Ariel to meet her dad. When Ariel and I arrived, he was not there. He showed up late, and when he did, he had a woman in the car with him. I said a few choice words to him, "Your priorities are never in the right place," or something along those lines. I did not care that he had a woman with him; hell, it seemed like I drove a great distance to meet him, and then he was late and had a woman with him! Ok, maybe that made me a little mad, but it was just selfish of him. You had time to pick her up or whatever, but you could not be on time to pick up your daughter? Oh ok. The exchange was made. I kissed my baby goodbye for a while and drove like I had police escorts back to Fort Stewart before the commander knew I was gone. Thank God that I made it back safely. I was still covered even when I was not following the straight and narrow path.

One of the challenges I faced at Fort Stewart was getting in trouble for falsifying a government document and submitting it to my leasing office in Savannah, Georgia. What had happened was that I was living on one income, providing for my daughter, and commuting back and forth from Savannah to Hinesville daily. I was stressed out. As a platoon leader, I was at PT formations on time, and I stayed late as needed to close out daily tasks. As a mother, I woke my daughter up at 3 am daily, got her ready, got myself ready, drove to Hinesville, dropped her off at daycare as soon as it opened, and then rushed to the 0630 formation. This happened five days a week! Then, at the end of the day, I would pick Ariel up and drive back to Savannah.

I did all of this on a 2nd Lieutenant's pay. Not much was left once food, daycare, pull-ups, gas, rent, and expenses were compiled. Because we were in the era of rapid deployments, a brigade was always deploying out of Fort Stewart. One of my lieutenant friends, who was in another brigade gave me the idea to use another brigade's orders to break my lease in Savannah that I was paying $927 monthly to move to Hinesville and pay $680 monthly. Before I took any action on what she recommended, I talked to my company commander to tell him about my financial problems and to see if he could write me a letter to break my lease and move close to post or on post. He did not write me a letter. He was adamant that it would not help me. He never referred me to Army Community Service for help, nor did I know about it. So, I was back to the idea my friend had. She helped me construct the orders. I submitted it to my leasing office so I would not have to pay to break the lease. Well, the leasing office found out. They did not tell me, but they reported me straight to my chain of command.

My company commander and I had to go and see the battalion commander. The battalion commander was this little short man who loved making examples out of people and had a country accent for a Caucasian male. The first thing he asked me was if I did it. I told him, "Yes, sir, I did." He told me that I do amazing work with my platoon and in the battalion. He just knew that my husband (he didn't know we were getting a divorce) had falsified the document and not me. He told me that my mama would not be proud of my actions. I had no idea where that comment came from because I had a daddy, too, but it did upset me. He never asked me why I did it. Had he asked me, I would have told him everything and the part about me asking my company commander (who stood behind me and said nothing the entire time) for assistance with the matter. I received a Letter of Reprimand, and it was filed locally. I did not quite understand what this would mean for my career, but it devastated me, and I just knew that my career was over.

Killa asked me why I didn't tell on the company commander and the other people who helped me with the fake orders. I did not want to get my friend in trouble. It was her idea, but I did not have to go along with it. The truth is, I was desperate, and I needed something to happen soon. No one back home would have been able to help me with my finances, so

I never brought it up. I also had too much pride to admit that I was not good with money or needed help across the board. Being a single mom in the military was not easy. The truth was that I was going to have to send Ariel back to my parents to take care of. We were informed that our brigade was getting ready to deploy, and I was barely making it as it was. One thing we have in military communities is our military families, whom we meet along the way. A few families helped me with Ariel when I had to go to the field or pull staff duty. Killa's girlfriend, Carolina, loved Ariel and helped me out a lot. My JSU ROTC classmate, Rodney Freeman, and his beautiful wife, Calandra, helped me tremendously. Randalle also helped us when she could. We were blessed to have the right people in the right places to get through the hard times.

Ariel was now back in Mississippi with my parents. I was alone at Stewart and trying my best to cope with her not being with me and doing a good job as a platoon leader. I was so depressed and mentally drained. Other than Killa and Randalle, I didn't have many people to talk to. One day, I was told that I was on staff duty. I was not prepared for it. I can't remember how it came up, but I was literally at the motorpool, and when I got off work, I reported to the battalion for duty. The battalion commander had left for the day, thank God! I did not want to see him again. During the first five hours of my shift, an Infantry Soldier said he wanted to commit suicide. I called the chaplain and sat with the Soldier to talk with him until the Chaplain came. He had relationship issues and financial issues. He did not want to deploy. I understood where he was coming from. When the chaplain arrived, he took the Soldier into his care.

My platoon and I were busy training for our upcoming deployment to Iraq. We went to the National Training Center (NTC) in Fort Irwing, California, before leaving for Iraq. I was confident in my job as a platoon leader and the mission of my platoon. It was a good time to be a platoon leader! Mistakes happened, but I learned from them. We trained harder, and we got better. Killa and I created a family environment. We all looked out for each other. After all, we were about to go to another country where we would have to depend on one another for survival. We understood that.

At NTC, the females slept in the same clamshell tent as everyone else in our company. Our company was huge because we provided sustainment to all of the units in the Infantry Battalion. At the time, we only had about five females in my platoon and a total of fifteen in the Battalion. One evening after training, one of the females ran back into the tent, frightened by derogatory comments that were written on the porta potty. The chain of command was informed, but nothing happened. We made sure that we had a battle buddy with us if we were walking somewhere after that. To operate in fear not knowing who around you made the derogatory comments was enough to drive anyone crazy. The worst thing to do is lump everyone in the same category. But I must say, if other male soldiers were not in our platoon or company, we did not entirely trust them the same. This was not the first time something happened that made me, as a female, doubt the leadership and the safety of female soldiers who remain outnumbered in almost every military occupational skill and branch.

11

Psalm 91

I remember flying into Kuwait by plane. It was the longest ride ever. Cousin Troy and I woke up every so often and played spades with a few others, but eventually, we went back to sleep. On this long flight, I met Georgia Girl. The soldier sitting next to her did not shower or touch any water before he boarded the plane. She was over it. I looked over at one point and asked her what was wrong, but then I smelled the same thing that caused her face to frown the way she did. It was a long ride, and Georgia Girl and I were cool from then on. She was not in my company, but I saw her later during deployment at another Forward Operating Base (FOB). My platoon and I stayed in Kuwait for a few days to get acclimated before we flew to Iraq. When the time came to hurry up and wait to get on the chinook, my heart raced. My head was spinning a bit, but I played it off and kept my cool. All I could think about was the "what ifs." What if I did not make it back home to Ariel? What if all the training we did does not keep us from losing a soldier? What if this damn chinook gets shot down on the way over there? I had so many discouraging thoughts that I darn near passed out with all my gear on. But there was no time to do that! We began a slow walk, single file, to get on the chinook. My platoon and I were headed to Forward Operating Base Iskan. All I could pray for was God's protection.

As the chinook took off, I took several deep breaths. We were packed in that chopper-like sardines. It had several seats in the middle and seats on the sides. I had no idea how long the flight was into Iraq, but my nerves were very bad. I began to hear my mama's voice as she quoted Psalm 91. It became my scripture and prayer to guide me through my entire deployment. Some refer to Psalm 91 as "The Soldier's Prayer." I heard my dad's voice echo, "You can do anything; you're a Harvey." The back door opened a little, and we were able to see the terrain leading into FOB Iskan. There were many lights, but then there were only a few. It was quiet. Everything was still. We were briefed on light and noise discipline prior to deplaning. We landed, got off, and went into a building for a briefing and to get assigned quarters. I was so glad to get to my room and drop all my gear. Our females stayed in two rows, and our latrine was not too far from our rooms. FOB Iskan was rocky, hot, and quiet. But we knew we were being watched and would not stay that way for long.

When people in the Army say, a deployment is what you make it or a duty station is what you make it, that's just what we mean! Being without Ariel and not knowing if I was going to make it back to her or not was nerve-wracking. The first thirty days, I darn near cried myself to sleep every night. I did not want to be there. I did not want anything to happen to any of my soldiers under my watch. It was a lot to take on mentally. But I put my best face forward when I stepped out of my room. No one knew how I truly felt. I did not look it. I did not carry it on my shoulders. I appeared like I was all in. I was ready for whatever might happen daily since each day was a mystery. On one of the Infantry's patrols, we lost SGT Kelsey to an IED. Then, later at the outpost, we lost SSG Dawson to another soldier shooting him. To this day, I still do not know what really happened to SSG Dawson, but it stunned us all. Then a week or two later, one of my older-Caucasian female soldiers accused one of my older-African American NCOs of assaulting her.

There were several speculations about this incident. I never chose sides and I heard the entire story, but SHARP was not too standard at the time, and we all messed up the reporting based on who needed to know. I do not even think CID was called. But I do know that her story kept changing, and the NCO she was accusing did not appear to be or do what she conveyed. After the female soldier told the battalion commander her story (that changed again, and she added tears this time), he sent her out and immediately called in my NCO. He had no idea what she had said, and we could tell. He just knew he could no longer talk or engage with the soldier. He answered the commander's questions and then got hammered because he did. It seemed like he complied and said 'yes' because the commander was yelling at him. The sad thing about this misfire sexual assault case is that it cost my NCO his career. He was punished because he admitted to whatever he thought she said and his career ended as a Sergeant.

The female soldier was immediately moved to another FOB, FOB Kalsu, where her husband was stationed. This baffled me. It could've been perceived as picking an easy target, breaking him down to believe he did cross the line, put on a full show, and then get what you wanted in the first place, which was to be moved closer to your husband. Wow! Did she really get assaulted? Who knows, but a career was surely ended. Sexual assault in the military is serious. I was sexually assaulted. Yes, every case is different. Yes, it is usually someone you know. It is not up to me to decide someone's fate when the proper steps were not taken. If anything, all the facts and testing should have been done before making a decision. I learned then, that at the end of the day, people take care of who they want to take care of. It was a hard lesson to learn at the expense of someone else's livelihood.

On FOB Iskan, my platoon ran a fuel farm and ammunition holding area. Just as we were getting the hang of our mission, I was informed that I would be moving from the Distribution Platoon Leader to the company's Executive Officer (XO). This was bittersweet. But it made sense. A week before this move was made, the battalion commander held a quick formation and lined all of us second lieutenants up. He pinned us all as first lieutenants, and then we got right back to work. Because we were deployed, we did not have large formations, only small gatherings. That was my second pinning and promotion as an officer, and I did not get to say anything, nor did my family see it. However, I called my parents and told them about my promotion. I also told them about my new position. Surprisingly, as the XO, I had way more free time than I did as the platoon leader. I had meetings to attend with the Battalion XO and other company XOs, but it was nothing hard. I missed my platoon because that is who I had trained and bonded with. Being the XO allowed me time to roam around the FOB, meet others, and learn different jobs and skills.

I met a group of Reserve Unit NCOs and soldiers who ran the shower, laundry, and sewing facility for FOB Iskan. They were true professionals and always met customers with a smile. We attended some of the same meetings and briefings and played spades often. Their female NCO was among the other African American senior NCOs on the FOB. Before leaving FOB Iskan and relocating to FOB Kalsu, they made me a personalized laundry bag. That was the kind of relationship I had with them.

Although they were in my company already, I absolutely loved our Cooks (92Gs). They ran a professional Dining Facility in the middle of the desert! On your way inside the DFAC, a menu with an encouraging quote for the day was displayed. They always played music, and everyone smiled. The cooks were my favorite! I loved to eat, and they always made good food. I have no idea how they turned Army rations into gourmet meals, but they did. We also played spades a lot, and we sang in the FOB's Gospel Choir. The cooks did it all. A few were rappers, some were singers, and they were a force to reckon with in spades. Going to the DFAC took my mind off being deployed for a split second. What brought me back to where I was, of course, were the hesco concrete barriers and bunkers that you saw throughout the FOB, as well as everyone carrying their weapons at the ready wherever they went.

As the XO, I sometimes borrowed the gator and rode out to the fuel point and ammunition holding area (AHA) to check on my soldiers. They always rotated people out for different shifts and allowed soldiers a chance to get downtime and call home. Cousin Troy at the AHA always had a game of spades going. Yes, if you have not figured it out by now, it was either spades or dominoes happening simultaneously throughout the day during deployment. He taught me the process of ammunition accountability, and I watched him issue rounds from time to time. He ended up being my spades partner. He did most of the trash-talking, and I came through like the silent killer that I was. Meanwhile, Berta worked at the fuel point. Berta was my sister. From day one, she and I talked about everything. She told me when I was screwing up as a platoon leader, officer, etc. She always kept it real with me, and I could talk to her without our conversations going around the FOB. Berta did not know it then, but she kept me out of a lot of trouble. Yes, I was a little mischievous, but I also cared about people and how I treated them.

As a female officer, as a female, period, you only get one reputation. When people hear your name, it will either be good or bad, with no in-between. I was fortunate not to get caught up in any foolishness. There were times when God removed me from situations so that I did not mess things up for myself.

One of my stops also included the maintenance bays. That's where Cousin Daley and Light-Skin worked. Those two together were hilarious. They had a crazy warrant officer and a silly Battalion Maintenance Officer (BMO), but I made it work. The warrant officer and the BMO did not particularly like me, but I knew where to go to get good information for my meetings. It pays to have connections across the board. It was NCOs that showed me how to read the maintenance report correctly. Networking was 98% of being an XO. I obtained the information I needed to get the resources the battalion needed whenever our logistics packages (LOGPACs) were pushed to us from the Brigade Support Battalion. Whenever a LOGPAC came, I made sure that I was there to receive it with the Battalion S4, Cousin Troy, and our fuelers.

SGT Wright was our supply sergeant, and he always had stuff coming on the LOGPAC. He was the first supply sergeant I encountered in my career. He was a Caucasian male who sounded like an African American when he talked. He was different but fun and fair. SGT Wright could get you anything you needed. He always "knew a guy!" As a Platoon Leader and an XO, I always worked with SGT Wright. As a platoon leader, I was signed for property. As an XO, I was ensuring that everything was managed properly. SGT Wright was good with paperwork, and he trained his two supply clerks well. Overall, we had a good team. I did not particularly care for my company commander at the time because he did not help me when I needed him the most. He also did not stand up for me when I was at my lowest point, yet I remained loyal to the unit and its overall success.

My shady company commander left, and a new one came to FOB Iskan to take his place. He was also a Caucasian male. He had a really huge lemon head and a weird voice. He was from Buffalo, New York. He teased me about being from Mississippi and talking with a slow accent. I asked him why did they have rats on every corner in New York. We both laughed, and the rest was history. He was much better than my previous company commander. I learned from the new commander that you cannot and should not judge a book by its cover. Other people may have wronged you or didn't look out for you like you thought they should, but you should not hold that against everyone who looks like them. I received initial counseling from my new company commander.

He understood my position as a mother and my grooming needs as an African American female when it came to my hair. Yes, it sounds weird, but if my hair was jacked up, then it would be a long day for everyone. My commander literally approved for me as the XO to go on convoys to FOB Kalsu to let one of his former NCOs, SSG Harvey, do my hair. The irony is that my name was 1LT Harvey at the time. When I met SSG Harvey, she was like my cousin in real life! From that point on, she and her battle buddies always looked out for me. SSG Harvey worked in the Support Operations Shop and sometimes in the SSA at FOB Kalsu. She was a joy to be around.

One of the biggest lessons I learned from deploying to Iraq was that change does not have to be bad or automatically assumed that you did something wrong. Over halfway into the deployment, after receiving my new company commander, he told me that a new XO was coming to take my place. I was so confused because what was I supposed to do now? He explained that I was moving to FOB Kalsu to work in the Mayor Cell for CPT Stinnie and also to be reunited with my former Platoon Sergeant, Killa. That part I was excited about. Every time I went to FOB Kalsu on convoys, I saw Killa. All of our soldiers missed him, and we would go to the DFAC on FOB Kalsu together. It was bittersweet to leave FOB Iskan, the place where I first landed in Iraq—the place where I changed duty positions and was living my best life. But the truth was that I was getting too comfortable. When you are deployed, the last thing you want to do is get too comfortable.

Going to the Mayor Cell was a new experience for me across the board. I had no idea what I was going to be doing. The only good news Killa told me was that I would have my own room again. I also had my own room at FOB Iskan, so that was a plus. He told me that I would be one of the few LTs with my own room on the FOB and not to broadcast that. In fact, everyone at the Mayor Cell had their own rooms. It was only a handful of people. After arriving and saying goodbye to my former company, I met CPT Stinnie, who was a hoot. The man was stupid smart. He worked like a robot. He was always busy, gave quick instructions, and kept it moving. Killa told me how to maneuver around him and ensure that I met his intent. So, I did as he suggested. CPT Stinnie made me a Field Ordering Officer, and Killa was the Pay Agent. I was also in charge of MWR events on FOB Kalsu and new construction projects through the LOGCAP program. I had to quickly learn how to review contracts and ensure that the scope of work was clear regarding what we (the government) were asking the contractor to do. Killa often helped me tweak those documents before handing them over to CPT Stinnie. I was doing ok with my new duty position. I still felt at first like I had done something wrong and had to be moved, but I knew that my company commander would have told me the truth if I did.

At FOB Kalsu, I was reunited with Randalle and a few others I knew in the 703rd Brigade Support Battalion. It was like a darn family reunion over there. I left one family and came to another one. They embraced me, and all was well until I realized that nobody liked the Mayor Cell or any of us who worked there. Killa tried to explain it to me several times. It was useless. We clearly had it too good at the Mayor Cell, and other people were a little jealous, I guess. CPT Stinnie did not care what people said or thought. He kept hitting home runs. That was the genius thing about him.

One day, I went to lunch with a few of my LT friends, and a few weeks later, I had a new roommate scheduled to move in with me, and I was put in the rotation to run LOGPACs. I was pissed at first, but then I realized it was all good getting off the FOB every now and then. I took my duty as a convoy commander seriously. The gun truck crews were from either HHC or Alpha Company, but they were solid. They taught me everything I needed to know as the truck commander, and I had no problem briefing my OPORD and confirming all loads before each mission. I actually enjoyed being a convoy commander whenever my name came up in the rotation. By doing this, I got a chance to go to other FOBs that I never would have gone to. I also got to see one of my battle buddies at one of the other FOBs. I was getting the hang of juggling many duties and excelling at them all.

Then, one day, one of our regular local nationals wanted to thank us for all of the business and support he had been receiving and he brought three big flat-screen televisions onto the FOB. I did not think much about it. He had been working with me and Killa. I initially accepted the television from him, but when I thought about it, I decided to have him take it back. At this point, I was already preparing for my new roommate to move in, and that tv was huge. Little did I know, Killa was right; we, "The Mayor Cell," had haters.

One of the NCOs who knew Killa called CID and opened up a whole investigation about receiving gifts as payment or whatever the allegation was. He and I both had to talk to CID separately. I was mad that the attention was now on all of us at the Mayor Cell, but I was honest with CID. Yes, I initially took the tv, but I also gave it back. I did not have that tv any time. It came and left the same day, and Killa gave his back, too. Neither of us was scheming for money or taking gifts. As the Pay Agent, Killa's count and paperwork were always correct. He signed for money, issued it out, and tracked it. He was really good with paperwork. All 92As were. CPT Stinnie also had our backs when CID interviewed him.

No one was doing shady stuff. Seriously, why would anyone want to risk their career over foolishness? I called on the only one who could make things right, and that was God. I prayed Psalms 91 relentlessly, "He is my refuge and my fortress; My God; in him will I trust.... For he shall give his angels charge over thee, to keep thee in all thy ways." Time went on, and the case was closed. We were all devastated but moved on to continue providing what the FOB needed. The messed-up part about doing well in a position is that you can do a thousand good things, but if you do one wrong thing, that is what everyone remembers. It's like the thousand good things never happened. And with that, Killa and I did not receive Meritorious Service Medals for our tour in Iraq. After all the hard work and projects we did and my time in 3-7 Infantry Battalion, we received Army Commendation Medals. I learned several hard lessons from that. As an officer, an award will not depict who you are and what you deserve. When I saw my Officer Evaluation Report (OER) from CPT Stinnie, I learned what really mattered. He knew that we were probably going to get screwed on those awards, but he wrote my truth on my OER. Giving credit where credit is due goes a long way with me. I do not care if you do not like someone; if they are professional, respectful, meeting your intent, and doing their best to effect change, you should give them the write-up they deserve. If you did not take the time to counsel them and allow them time to make the necessary adjustments in order to be number one, then you are doing them an injustice as their rater and senior rater. I knew that God had placed the right people in the right places for me, and His will for me was done.

12

Rough Rider 6

My 13-month tour in Iraq had finally come to an end. After returning to Fort Stewart, I was a few months away from pinning on captain. I visited the Battalion S1 and asked her about attending the Captains Logistics Career Course (CLC3). She looked me in my face and told me I could not attend because I was not a captain yet. I did not like her answer because I was promotable, and to my understanding, that's all I needed to qualify to go. My friend, Randalle, was also promotable, and she had gotten a slot. She had not yet pinned captain. She told me to call our branch officer directly, so I did. I reached a civilian who asked me one question after I told him what my unit S1 had told me. He asked me when I wanted to attend. I told him as soon as possible! I out-processed Fort Stewart and began my journey to Fort Gregg-Adams (former Fort Lee), Virginia. When I completed my leave and reported to CLC3, my Leave and Earnings Statement (LES) said Captain, so I put my captain rank on. After the way my promotion to first lieutenant had gone in Iraq, I figured it was fine to just put my rank on and keep it moving.

The good thing about CLC3 was that my teacher, MAJ Youngblood, was cooler than a fan. He told us what we needed to know and he did not care about running us into the ground. He had an injury and no longer ran. One of my sorority sisters was in my section with MAJ Youngblood. Her name is LaTecia McGrady. She was squared away. Between her, Al, Mike, Marissa, Deatae, and Brian, we made it through CLC3. I did not realize it at the time, but most of my classmates were in the 2005 year group. I was in the 2006 year group. I was quiet in class.

I did not like to yell out answers or be put on the spot. I preferred to stay to myself. When I was in CLC3, I was close to completing my Masters in Business Administration. Unlike my other classmates, I had a lot going on. I was so stressed out that I almost failed my darn APFT run. I barely made the cut-off, and even the time was up for debate because it was on the line. But thank God I was good to go. I vowed to never be in that situation again. I was short but stout, so my height and weight never matched. I always had to get taped. I passed, but it was always so nerve-wracking. I knew that I was Mississippi-grown. Some of the distinct features in my figure were not going anywhere; they would always be a part of me.

In CLC3, I decided to train to get my Combative Level I certification. Randalle was in the CLC3 class before mine, and she told me what to expect, so I got to it. The funniest thing about the certification was the clinch drill at the end. It was like lining up to get punched in the head for the world to see. I must admit, watching so many people go through and get punched before my turn was so intimidating. Most people, however, were able to achieve the clinch their second time. When it was my turn, I decided to use my height to my advantage when approaching my opponent. I got punched so hard in my face mask. That did not work at all. I side-stepped a bit but stayed on my feet; by that time, I was pissed anyway, so I rushed in fast and achieved the clinch. Yeah, I was not for anyone hitting me in my face, mask or no mask.

Nearing the end of CLC3, Randalle had told me she was going to Fort Cavazos (former Fort Hood), Texas, for company command. She was from Texas and always wanted to be near her family. I, of all people, understood that. After all, Killeen was like a seven-hour drive from Jackson, Mississippi. I figured I could do that in my sleep. Randalle told me about a company that was opening in Texas, but I was battling with wanting to return to Fort Stewart and be an FSC Company Commander. I thought that it was what I wanted and needed to remain competitive. While trying to figure it out, Randalle put me in touch with the Battalion Commander she knew from FOB Kalsu, who was also in 703rd BSB when we were all there in Iraq and back at Stewart. I emailed him first, told him about Randalle, and asked about the command. He told me to call him. I called him, and I was set to go to the 589th BSB to take company command.

I was one class away from completing my master's in business administration, and my statistics class gave me pure hell. The textbook and help sites were not working for me. One day in class, I shared my struggle with Deatae, and he picked me up by my boot straps and helped me get on the right track to close out statistics. Thank God for Deatae because I was set to walk the stage and graduate with my master's degree in the spring. I could actively see things working together for my good. Graduation from CLC3 was upon us, and my battle, Brian Stanfield, was getting promoted. He had the Quartermaster General at the time to promote him, and he was African American. I was impressed. It was the first time I had seen something like this. I forgot that I had told Brian about pinning my rank on before signing in to CLC3, and he told this General. After Brian's ceremony and we congratulated him, the General did a quick impromptu ceremony for me. I was shocked! I appreciated it so much. Brian fussed at me again and then congratulated me, too. After that act of kindness, I never took another promotion for granted. It was a privilege. I deserved it and vowed to celebrate it from that point forward.

After leaving Fort Gregg-Adams, Virginia, I took leave to spend time with Ariel and my family before signing in at Fort Cavazos. It was a much-needed break. Whenever I went back home to Mississippi, I would always call up a few friends, and after Ariel went to bed, I'd step out to Freelon's The Groove for a few hours. At home was the only place I could really let my hair down and be in good company. The majority of my time at home was dedicated to Ariel. She was now three going to four and she loved Chuck E. Cheese. I did, too. I was glad we could venture off with Bugg and get into mischief at the County Fair and other places when I was home.

When I reported to Fort Cavazos, I worked initially in the Support Operations (SPO) Cell as the SPO Deputy. My boss was an African American female Major with an annoying voice and laugh. She was from Boston. I never did anything to this woman, but she did not like me for some reason. She always had caddy comments. She always bragged about herself and said mean things about others around her. I never stayed in her presence long. She told the Battalion Commander that I was not ready to be a company commander. He told her that I was and that it was happening. Before my battalion commander assigned me a company, he asked me what type of company I wanted. I told him I wanted an FSC. So, he sent me for an interview. My battle buddy Josh also interviewed for the same FSC. Josh got it. I took Alpha Company, the Distribution Company in the 41st Fires Brigade. I was bummed and happy at the same time. What I thought I wanted was not what God intended for me. Alpha Company Rough Riders was exactly where I was supposed to be. And so, I became Rough Rider 6!

As the new Rough Rider 6, I received a good handoff from my predecessor. When it came to property and inventories, I had a new supply sergeant who had been transferred to me from HHC. That was fine with me. SGT Witcher was good at her job but had several other personal things she was also trying to balance. We conducted my incoming 100% inventory of the company's property. Everything that I annotated as a shortage was supposed to be ordered throughout my tenure so that I would be good to go once my time in command was over. However, none of the shortages were ever ordered, and when I changed command, I had over a $2.5 million FLIPIL. In my mind, I had done everything right. I completed my monthly cyclic inventories and always annotated when the equipment was moved or laterally transferred to someone else. I was always in touch with the Brigade PBO. The biggest piece that I was missing was the level of understanding of how to use PBUSE and how to ensure parts were being reordered. My incoming Brigade Commander gave me a break because I explained it all to him, and so did the Brigade PBO. I was very proactive when managing property, but I did not have the expertise to pinpoint when things were not done quite right in the system. I probably should have been relieved, but the nation was in constant war and money was abundant. I was selected to serve as the Brigade S4 after completing company command, and I was not happy about that. I had no idea what the Brigade S4 was supposed to be doing. And I certainly did not want anything to do with property. But I'll get back to that in a minute.

As a company commander, I had a really strong XO that came to replace the current one. 2LT Johnson was from Alabama and he was soft-spoken but applied lots of logic and knew how to get things done. 2LT Harris was my Fuel & Water platoon leader. He was prior service and a Stanford graduate. He took the lead on many of our company projects and ways to reinvent ourselves. Because I was a single mom at the time of company command, I was grateful for 2LT Harris and SSG Naccarato to spearhead our Family Readiness Group. Their platoon went to Fort Gregg-Adams for actual water training and testing using the ROWPU and TWPSS.

My SSA platoon leader was 2LT Kuziel. He was bright-eyed and bushy-tailed. He was a good asset to the team. When I received the phone call that he had gotten a DUI, I had to go pick him up from the MP Station. It was not a good feeling, but he had to be removed as a platoon leader after that. One of the things I regret with 2LT Kuziel is that as a young company commander, I did not realize that as an officer facing a General Letter of Reprimand, I should have advised LT to write a letter explaining what happened and how he'd learned from his mistakes. Instead, I told him he probably should not say anything because it was like admitting guilt. That was the worst advice I could've ever given someone in trouble. After all, as an LT, I had gotten in trouble, too, and had been given another chance. When the new Brigade Commander called me in his office about LT's case, I had already changed command and was working as the Brigade S4. He asked me why I advised the LT not to say anything, and I explained to him that I did not quite understand the process and that I should have sought more legal counsel before advising the LT. I was scolded a bit, but I was dismissed without any backlash.

There were so many crazy things happening during my company command that I could hardly keep up. It took my First Sergeant about four months to understand that the things I was doing and the changes I made were for the company's overall good. For example, my predecessor left me with several Article 15 and chapter packets to close out. Well, I could not just punish or process a Soldier out without hearing their part of the story, so that took me the first three months of command to complete with the help of my First Sergeant. Before every ruling, I would ensure that I spoke to legal after hearing the Soldier's story. In some cases, the First Sergeant agreed with me, and in other cases, she did not.

Unlike most leaders back then, I believed in second chances because someone had given me one. So, I was not quick to severely punish a soldier or to put them out of the Army without understanding their financial and family situations. Maybe I was too soft to some, but to me, I was reasonable. A company commander has a lot of power to influence and change a person's livelihood, and I did not take that lightly. I bumped heads with my first sergeant about being too far into soldiers' personal businesses. She made it her business to speak Spanish with

Spanish-speaking soldiers when other people who did not speak Spanish were around. My first sergeant was older than me and, to most people I looked like one of the soldiers. I respected my first sergeant until I realized that she thought I was slow. My SSA Warrant Officer told me to watch out for her and the rumors that she began to spread or tried to. The crazy thing is that the soldiers were so crazy about me and the changes I brought about that they did not care what she had to say, nor did they repeat any of that foolishness.

One of the biggest lessons I learned about counseling was from my First Sergeant. One day, she had absolutely crossed the line. I had made my mind up, and it was time to counsel her. I typed out my DA Form 4856, walked into her office, and told her I wanted to counsel her. She looked at me and said, "Ma'am, that's not how that works. May I suggest you pick a date on the calendar and set up a time and location away from the company to conduct the counseling?" I was flabbergasted! I was so hot with that woman! However, not tying emotions to the situation, I realized that she was correct when I walked back to my office. Counseling should not be done when you are upset with someone. Counseling should be scheduled and done in a neutral place. It also taught me that most senior leaders understand what they need to do and what's expected of them, but a conversation still needs to happen and be written down for both parties to revisit later. Counseling can almost be thought of as a contract.

Initial counseling is the most important form of counseling. It is an open conversation to get to know each other, to understand what is expected, and the best ways to move things forward for the growth of the individual and the organization. I had no problems counseling everyone else, but my First Sergeant was the most challenging. So, with that, it did take us a while to get on the same page. But when we did, we were unstoppable. We were the only female command team in our brigade at the time. We had the highest re-enlistment rates, highest PT scores, best cadence callers, and best timing on awards and NCOER submissions. The Rough Riders were true professionals with stellar NCOs, Officers, and Soldiers.

I learned so many lessons from company command. First, I was blessed to have a battalion commander who allowed me the freedom and flexibility to command my company without interference. He trusted that I had it, and I proved that I did. I learned that leaders have to be about what they are talking about. I loved and cared for my soldiers and leaders. I was probably pretty hands-on to the point where they saw me everywhere, but it was more so that I understood how my company was doing. Soldiers could walk up and talk to me. I was in the motorpool for maintenance on Mondays and for closeout on Fridays. The one time I was late to the motorpool was when my previous Brigade Commander stole my HMMWV and drove it up to my office. I was so embarrassed. All the time, I was where I needed to be; the one time I was late, he showed up. There was no excuse. Each time my previous Brigade Commander showed up for our morning PT sessions, I ensured I ran with my A Group runners. I made sure to rotate running groups. It seemed like we ran almost daily. But one of my favorite run days was Fridays because it was when I would lead my company on runs. Some of the Soldiers hated it, and some loved it. Personally, I hated running, but I loved to run and call cadence with my soldiers. They motivated me to want to run, be better, try harder, and keep them motivated. It is hard to explain, I was not the fastest, but I always tried my best.

I must admit that I was a work-alcoholic, but I did not go to any meetings to deem me so. I had no idea what work and life balance even meant. My First Sergeant and XO finally convinced me to take some leave. It was so hard for me to unplug. During my command, Ariel lived in Mississippi and attended New Hope Christian Academy. So, I decided to take their advice and go on leave for a few days. When I came back, my XO broke the news that someone had stolen my guidon. I was furious!

My supply sergeant had to order another one. We laughed about it after the fact, but at the time, I was super hot! It was one of the few times I lost my cool.

During one of our battalion field training exercises, the weather had gotten really bad and damaged a lot of equipment. The battalion did not pull us out of the storm that was happening; we all hunkered down in the field. The First Sergeant and I stayed in the same tent. Out of nowhere, 2LT Harris and 2LT Johnson ran up to our tent in the rain, explaining that the storm had blown their tent away. My initial response was, "So, y'all just let my tent blow away? That's on my property book!" 2LT Harris said, "Um, ma'am, we are ok, though." I quickly regrouped, "LT, I'm glad y'all are ok. Please just get out of the rain." It was the second time I had lost my cool. The next day, they all laughed at me so hard. I was shell-shocked about the darn property book. I was glad that my LTs were ok. They, after all, were great leaders, and I was glad they understood who I was as a leader. At the end of the day, when you work hard and begin to see those you lead go off and do great things or run into them again in their civilian occupations, and they are doing well, it is all worth it. My goal is to always leave a unit or organization better than how I found it.

As previously mentioned, after completing fifteen months of company command, I was selected to be the Brigade S4 as a captain. The major that was there was deploying to Afghanistan. I already knew I would not be in the position long. I had orders to move to Camp Shelby, Mississippi, for my post-command job. Mentally and physically, I had short-timer syndrome, but the moment I met the Brigade S4 Team, I felt at home. Together, we rebuilt the relationship gaps that the team was receiving from some of the company commanders throughout the brigade. In one of my first meetings with the Brigade Commander, staff, battalion commanders, and company commanders, one of the company commanders commented on my budget slide while I was briefing it and made it seem like I was throwing him under the bus about his portion of the budget. He didn't know that in everything that I sent to each of them, I copied my shop and blindly copied the Brigade XO. I let him finish, and then I explained to the Brigade Commander, not to the company commander, but to the Brigade Commander, that I emailed all of the command teams their budgets and instructed them to respond by a no later than time (that I determined) with any need to increase their allocated amount and that I would work it from there. Only two company commanders reached out to me, and he was not one of them. Pending your questions Sir! When I tell you, you could've heard a pen drop!

The Brigade Commander said, roger that. Let's move on. I never had a problem with that specific company commander again or anyone else for that matter. In a short time, I helped the team repair its image, redefined its processes with managing the budget and reports, developed a good working relationship with the Division G4, and closed out several FLIPILs across the brigade. My NCOIC was an African American woman, well in her 40s. At first glimpse, she looked at me as a baby. Once I got into action, she knew I was mature for my age. She was happy to have me, and the shop was sad to see me go when the time came. I must leave this chapter with the famous saying, "Do not judge a book by its cover!"

13

First In Deed

My adventures in First Army is where I began to see how things can change the trajectory, like how Kobe tore his ACL in the middle of the game, shot his own free throws, and then painfully walked off the court! Rest In Heaven, Black Mamba! I must say, it was very odd to my branch manager for me to ask for Camp Shelby, Mississippi! The funny thing is how I chose it. I saw Camp Shelby on the list and called my branch manager. He said, "If you want it, it's yours. I don't see you competing with anyone for that duty station." After my Brigade S4 time, I was headed to Camp Shelby, MS. I went to Jackson first because that's where Ariel lived with my parents and her Uncle Bugg. I was so happy to be stationed at Camp Shelby because it was the closest duty station I could serve near my daughter and my family. I loved everything about Camp Shelby. I played softball on my breaks and after work. I was off work by 1430 every day and didn't go back to work after lunch on Fridays. On most Fridays, I drove back to Jackson to see my family.

At Camp Shelby, I was the assistant Brigade S4 in the 177th Armored Brigade Combined Arms Training Brigade (CATB). The Brigade S4 was a major and came in shortly after I did to the unit. He went to all the meetings. I made sure he had everything he needed prior to each meeting. Two of the new programs I learned as the assistant S4 back then was how to use Wide Area Workflow (WAWF) and the General Fund Enterprise Business System (GFEBS). After a few mistakes here and there, good NCOs squared me away, as always. First Army was a different animal; it was nothing like the 3rd Infantry Division or III Corps. The Brigade was always conducting the Military Decision-Making Process (MDMP) on the outcomes and training for upcoming unit rotations. I learned a lot about what a staff member's estimates meant and how they were integrated into the overall plans for mission execution. The unique thing about serving in this type of unit is that it consisted of both Active Component (AC), Reserve Component (RC) Officers and NCOs, and civilians. This working environment was less stressful than most until a mission came around.

At this duty station, I was selected to go to NTC as support staff and a Contracting Officer Representative (COR). Halfway through my mission in California, the major called me and told me that an individual deployment tasker had come down, and either he or I was going. I was waiting on the punch line. Of course, he had already volunteered for me to go. This type of deployment that I was informed about while actively on a mission meant that I would have to pack my household goods, drop my car off, and fly to the deployment mobilization center before heading to Afghanistan. The deployment needed a logistics advisor for either the Afghan National Army or the Afghan National Police. So I prepared to leave NTC and head back to Camp Shelby to prepare for deployment. What upset me was that no one could make a decision about when I was supposed to leave California to prepare for Afghanistan.

Time was ticking, and nothing was being coordinated by Camp Shelby. So, me being me, I packed up and left NTC and made it back to Camp Shelby to begin outprocessing and deployment preparations. I was at Camp Shelby for three days when I was informed that I needed to fly back to NTC to close out the contracts for the training units. Seriously!!!

So, can no one else handle that? Going on this individual deployment was stressful enough, and I had no idea where to begin. So I felt at that moment that I was being picked on. I was pissed. I did as I was told. I flew back to NTC. I closed out the supported units' contracts. I finished the rest of my time at NTC and flew back to Camp Shelby. By the time I returned to Camp Shelby, I had two months left before I was to report to the mobilization station. Wow!

Prior to leaving for this deployment, which would be my third time deploying and my second time to Afghanistan, I had mixed feelings about it. Financially, are deployments good, yes, but at what costs? I was not entirely sure that I would make it back by going on this deployment. After all, it was the first time I deployed alone, without an actual unit. With so many random thoughts in mind, I paid to store my household goods in Hattiesburg, Mississippi. I took both of my vehicles to my parent's house. I spent a few weeks with Ariel and my family. I even painted my parent's bedroom burgundy and yellow because I knew it was something my mom wanted done, and I wanted to leave her with her being happy. I flew to Fort Benning, Georgia, in the process of my individual deployment to Kabul, Afghanistan, for what I thought would be six months, but it was actually for twelve months. At Fort Benning, I ran into SFC P. She and I had deployed to Iraq in the 3rd Infantry Division. She worked in Alpha Company, 703rd BSB. We were glad to see each other. I also met a Chaplain's assistant who was also going to Afghanistan. It was us, and a few other ladies. We stuck together during processing and to the point when we boarded the plane. It felt good to be reassured that everything was going to be fine. I felt like God did this for me in so many ways leading up to this deployment.

Camp Phoenix was where I ended up during my Kabul, Afghanistan deployment. I was in processing with the unit in charge and met Heidi Kane, an Air Force Master Sergeant. She was my voice of reason, and she trained me on my new mission. We had so many mandates for what had to be transferred over to the Afghans that another team was standing up. Team Punisher, at least that's what we called ourselves. We consisted of two armored gun trucks. We had a major in charge of our team, and I was second in charge as the captain of the team. We went on missions every day. Every day, we were outside the wire in Kabul, Afghanistan. Our mission was to work with and advise an Afghan Colonel from the Afghan National Army to close a logistics depot and properly inventory and sign for a container yard. Later, I was moved to another team that worked with the Afghan National Police Transportation Corps. On this team, I advised an Afghan General on all transportation matters and vehicle maintenance. Both of the teams I served on were awesome. I worked with Air Force NCOs, Marine NCOs and officers, and National Guard NCOs and Soldiers within a year in Kabul, Afghanistan. It was truly a rewarding experience. I learned a lot about myself as a leader. I learned how to communicate clearer intent. I learned that relationships matter. Family matters. I also learned that mental health matters.

This deployment was the first time that I had worked closely and in person with senior logisticians. The first brigade commander of Asian descent sat down with me and conducted my initial counseling. That was when I first arrived in the country. He asked me about my goals and plans while I was there for that year. Then he asked me what I planned to do in the Army and in my personal life. He shared books for me to read. He told me that whatever I aspired to be, I should be reading what those who I was aspiring to be like were reading. I never said anything to him about the possibilities of becoming a general officer one day, but that's the reading list that he shared with me. I was impressed that he saw that I would continue to great heights in the Army, no matter what those heights would be. At that point in my military career, I was too nervous to share my dreams with people because I really cared what people thought, and I'm sure it would've sent me in another direction. The second brigade commander I had during that same deployment brought a different energy with him. He was a Caucasian male. He was super tall and very outspoken. I only encountered him during meetings. He liked my briefing style, and he visited one of my sites once. He was impressed with me, so all I had to do was avoid trouble.

Camp Phoenix was small enough to know everyone but big enough not to have to see them every day. There were two places I enjoyed going. The Green Bean on a Friday night was Karaoke. I absolutely enjoyed Karaoke. The other place I loved was going to choir practice during the week and church on Sundays. Yes, I sang in the choir. Praise and worship have always been my way of entering into my special place with God. Through songs and scriptures, I know He sees me and understands me when I can't quite put things into my own words. I loved singing in the choir. When you're deployed, the choirs seem much different than back in the States. People are there singing their truths. They leave it all at the altar. My sister, Erika, was our choir director. Everyone knew Erika. She was the FOB Mayor unofficially! She led us and was always open to suggestions until we got a new choir director after she re-deployed. I led the song "I've Got a Testimony" by Rev. Clay Evans and the AARC Mass Choir. This song is my truth to this day. With tears and a smile, this song always brings me joy and reminds me of how grateful I am that God has brought me all this way. There are other songs we sang, such as "Grateful," "Awesome," and "Victory is Mine." There were so many more, but these rang loud and true when we would gather for rehearsals and then sing on Sunday mornings. When God gives you a gift or a testimony, the gift or testimony is not for you; it is for you to share with someone else. You never know who you are helping by being obedient. Often, I was not obedient enough to share my gift or testimony, but there were times when I did, and I was so glad when I did. I felt as if God himself were pleased.

14

Is There Really Gold Here?

As soon as I redeployed from Kabul, Afghanistan, I went back through Fort Bliss to outprocess and go back to Camp Shelby to clear. I was thankful I did not have to stay in the unit at Camp Shelby. I was happy for a new adventure at Fort Knox, Kentucky. When I arrived at Fort Knox, it was beautiful and in the middle of nowhere. As I drove up and down the post, I wondered, "Is there really gold here?" Fort Knox was guarded well, just like any other post I had been to, so I was curious about the gold. No, I was not going to "Set it Off." I just wanted to know. Before I began to in-process, my mama informed me that my daddy was going in for a check-up. After I started in-processing and meeting everyone from the unit, my mama informed me that my daddy had some type of mass in his brain and that it needed to be removed, according to the doctor. At that moment, I took a deep breath and told my mama I would call her back. While in-processing, I met the S4 NCOIC, but I did not meet the OIC; he was retiring soon and not really there a lot. So I explained to my S4 NCOIC that I needed to go to Mississippi to check on my daddy. At this time, I did not have Ariel with me yet. I had not even found a house yet. My S4 NCOIC was fine with it, and I left.

I drove 8 ½ hours to Mississippi to check on my daddy. By the time I arrived, the doctor had completed the surgery. I was able to go in to see him once he had woken up, and he kept twitching like something else was wrong. My mama said she'd noticed the twitching also. We spoke back to the doctor, and he decided to do another scan on daddy's brain. While we were waiting for an update, the unit called me. Apparently, I had missed a newcomer's brief that I was supposed to attend in person since I had already signed in and started in-processing. I explained to the unit what was going on and that I would not be back within the next day or so in order to attend the follow-up briefing.

The Major, the Brigade S4, who was retiring, got on the phone and told me that I needed to get back there now. By the sound of his voice, he was a Caucasian male. He sounded old and nasty on the phone. I explained to him what was going on with my daddy and that the S4 NCOIC was tracking. He told me that I had taken advantage of the S4 NCOIC and should not blame him. I was so lost. I asked the major if he had anything else. He said no, and I hung up. I was furious, and all I wanted to do was choke that man. I did not tell my mama what had happened, but she could tell something was wrong.

I decided to disobey the major's order and stay in Mississippi until a plan was in place to make sure my dad's twitching would stop or find out what was causing the issue. The doctor explained that some of the mass was left, and he was taking daddy back in for another surgery. Hours went by, and I was falling apart but trying to keep it together for my mama, Bugg, and Ariel. I was a little concerned about hanging up in that major's face, but not really. My family is more important than this job. I had already started thinking about other careers I'd like to pursue if the Army didn't work out to the point where I could retire. I had already thought about the worst-case scenario so I would not be caught off guard. Daddy's second surgery went well. While waiting for him to recover and wake up, Bugg and I left the hospital and decided to meet up with an old friend for lunch. That friend was Jonathan Van.

Bugg and I met him at Chili's to eat lunch. When he showed up, he had a big grin on his face. He had no idea I had Bugg with me. He dapped Bugg up and we all went inside. My friend Netta was our waitress at the time. She took care of us and we enjoyed a nice lunch. Jonathan and I had been friends for about ten years. We met in our old Reserve Unit. We never dated but would talk often. Even when I went on active duty, we remained in touch. He was always easy to talk to. I told him about my daddy and not much about what happened back at Fort Knox with my new unit, and he told me that he was breeding and selling bullies and pitbulls.

I already had Tyson, my teacup poodle, and Zeus, my Mini-Pinscher. I knew that if we got a pitbull or a bully, one or both puppies would have to go, lol. Long story short, Jonathan gave me a pitbull for Ariel. Ariel was crazy about her and named her Jordan. In fact, once daddy woke up, we snuck Jordan inside the hospital so daddy could see her. He was tickled. Jordan licked on him and started biting the covers. She was so spunky. I was happy to see the smile on my daddy's face and the fact that he was much better and no longer had twitching or slurred speech. He was back, ready to go home to recover, and that's what he did.

Once daddy was discharged and home to rest, I called Jonathan to thank Him again for Jordan and to give him an update on my daddy. I was getting ready to pack up and return to Fort Knox to face the major and other people at the unit. Jonathan and I decided to have breakfast before I left. It was good seeing him and talking to him. He always had me laughing. It was raining that day, and as I pulled off and got on the interstate, I felt like I could've just stayed there and talked to him all day.

I made it back to Fort Knox that night and went to the unit the next morning. The first person I saw was my S4 NCOIC. He told me what happened. I told him that it was fine. It is what it is. The major showed up to work later on that week. He said two or three words to me, and I never saw him again after that. Nothing ever came of me missing the newcomer's brief. I never understood why such a big deal was made like I was in trouble during a time when I was mentally and emotionally drained worrying about my daddy. I learned that the Brigade S4 position was going to be vacant, so I put my name in the hat. Looking across the brigade, I had the most experience as a captain, and I outranked the other Caucasian female captain that was also in our shop. She was prior Air Force and had a different year group than mine. So I thought it was a no-brainer. There was also another Caucasian guy, a logistician, who had just arrived at the unit, but he went to the S3 shop. I was not considered for the Brigade S4 position, but it was given to the other female captain that I outranked and had more experience than. Was it because of the way I entered the unit? Was it because I chose my family over the Army? Even if it was, my work ethic had nothing to do with caring for my family.

The fact that I was overlooked for the position when I had more experience, not once but twice, at the brigade level as an S4, was crazy to me. Normally, I would let things slide when people did stuff to me or against me because that's just how I was. But this didn't sit right with me at all. I opened the door with the Brigade Commander. He was also new to the unit, and neither he nor I was aware of how the unit was. Let me be frank: it was racist as hell. There have been times when I suspected that someone was racist, but in this unit, it was right in your face with no apology. During the open-door discussion, I only stated why I should be the Brigade S4 and only wanted to know why I was not considered. To this day, I do not remember what he told me, but he quickly moved me to the Brigade S3 shop to be the Logistics Plans Officer. So now I'm in the S3 shop, and I look like a troublemaker because I stood up for myself and was not ok taking a back seat to someone that I had more experience than. Looking back on it, I bet the Brigade Commander did not make the initial decision to put her in the seat, but I'm sure he knew that it would not be good for morale for me to stay in that shop and work under her. While all this was happening, I continued talking to my mama, Ariel, daddy, and Jonathan. In fact, I spoke to Jonathan almost every day when I got off work. It got to the point where I needed to hear his voice before I went to the office in the morning and before I went to bed at night. We had planned to get Ariel and Jya together the next time I was able to come home. So that's what I focused my energy on.

Time went by and in my new job as the Logistics Planner, we were preparing to go and be Observer Coach Trainers at Fort Johnson, Louisiana (formerly known as Fort Polk). The planning was going well. I was slated to go to the OC/T Academy before going on the mission. You won't believe where the OC/T Academy was. Oh yeah, it was at Camp Shelby, Mississippi. I was happy to go back for the training because I knew it was closer to Jonathan, but I didn't tell him that! Before my class, I went home for a weekend, and we got a chance to take Ariel and Jya to Chuck E. Cheese.

We had a good time. I took that opportunity to tell Jonathan about my training at Camp Shelby. He decided which days he could come and we had the best time. My former Brigade S4 NCOIC at Camp Shelby was still there, so he hooked me up with a room and a government vehicle to get around in while I was there for training. I only had my gear and equipment in the barracks with the other females, but I stayed in a VIP room with my Jonathan. It was meant to be! At one point, I was gone mostly one whole day for training, and I think he was locked in the room with nothing but Coop DeVille Wings (they are closed now due to racist remarks). He told me once I made it back to Fort Knox that what we had was what he'd been missing. I told him that he was what I needed. It was settled. We put a whole plan into motion!

I returned to Fort Knox from my training at Camp Shelby. I began preparing to go for temporary duty at Fort Johnson, Louisiana. Jonathan and I decided to get married before I headed off for my mission. We chose May 31, 2014, because it fell on Memorial day weekend, and more than likely, I would get three days or four days off to celebrate our future anniversaries. We chose to get married with a small group of our family and a few people from my unit. We decided to get married over a bridge and stream at Saunder's Spring Park, where we could stand in the stream and say our vows. We wanted nature around us. We chose to get married in the uniform that Jonathan never got to wear because he had been out of the Army before we changed to the digital pattern.

We wanted our flower girls, as well as a few of our family members, to wear little Army digital uniforms. We were bridging together two families in a military way of life. Our daughters read the scriptures that govern us and were instructed to hand us our wedding rings. We said our vows to each other and placed the rings on the proper fingers. We kissed and carefully stepped out of the stream. That was one of the happiest days of my life. My parents were happy. They had just traveled to Fort Knox and could not make it back for the wedding, but it was like they were there. This was a decision that my husband, Jonathan, and I made. It was not up for talking to anyone else about it. I always prayed for God to send me the man I am supposed to have. The man just for me. The person that I do not have to change anything about myself who would love me the way I am and grow with me. In every way, he inspired me. The summer after our marriage, I began working on my PhD, and he supported and encouraged me through it all. Jonathan was my answer to prayer, and on May 31, 2024, we celebrated in Waikiki, Hawaii, 10 years of marriage and loving each other.

15

Good Things Come to Those Who Wait

After our wedding, Jonathan, Ariel, and Jya held down the fort, and I went on my mission to Fort Johnson. We chose not to have a big wedding to save for our honeymoon in the Bahamas! That's right; we planned to take the girls with us so we could all experience a cruise and the Bahamas for the first time together. As soon as I returned from Fort Johnson, we left a few days afterward to go on our cruise to the Bahamas. We spent a week in the Bahamas. It was beautiful and serene. Ariel and Jya swam on the cruise ship prior arriving to the Bahamas. We walked to a nearby market and talked to some locals. We realized that Ariel had left her cell phone back in West Palm Beach, Florida, while we were in the Bahamas! Lol. We picked up her phone once we returned. It was a good time. I noticed some resentment from Ariel at times during the trip. But thinking back, Jonathan took time to explain to Jya how he felt about me and also asked her how she felt and what she thought about him marrying me. I did not do that for Ariel. I wish I had asked Ariel how she felt and what she thought. But communication was not my strong point then, and I thought it was, but it was not. We worked through our challenges as a blended family. I love Ariel and Jya the same way Jonathan does, as if we were supposed to be this way always. It just made sense, and nothing was forced.

My Brigade Commander did not know that I had put my honeymoon on hold to go on the mission to Fort Johnson. He began to see me in a new light, especially while I was handling the facilities' coordination and vehicles while there. My fellow captains and our one NCO were crushing it. We were all in the S3 shop except for our Brigade S1. But we all had each other's back. We were also all minorities. It's like the shop was split or something. It's hard to explain, but black people in a unit notice everything that happens or does not happen in terms of what and how things happen when it is a similar action for someone white. There, I said it. By being a woman, a black woman, you have to work even harder. You have to be physically fit. You can't take any shortcuts. So, regardless of who is watching me, I always put my best foot forward.

Most women get out of the Army because they want to start families or take care of the ones they have. Jonathan and I had been trying to get pregnant since we got married in May 2014. In October 2014, we were blessed with the news that we were pregnant! We already had two girls and prayed for a healthy baby boy to follow. When I was four months pregnant, a mission came up to travel back to Fort Johnson to OC/T a unit. I have no idea why certain individuals were not placed on the mission, but the major I worked for at the time asked me to go on the mission. His first mistake was that he asked me! There were other people to ask, why would you come and ask me, the four-month pregnant captain? Crazy enough, the Caucasian female captain who took over as the Brigade S4 (the job they did not want to give me) was also pregnant. I asked the major why I was being asked and she was not being asked. Is she not about four months pregnant also? There was a lot of back and forth.

Jonathan was two seconds from coming to my unit and going off on everyone. I knew that by doing that, it would just make things worse. I asked him to please let me work it out. Once again, I went to see the Brigade Commander on an open-door visit. He congratulated Jonathan and me on our pregnancy. Then he said, "Mia, if you do not want to go, that's fine. Someone else can go." I did not go. Once again, I was being eyeballed by the guys in the shop. I cannot expect them to care about me. Half of them did not care about their wives, those who were married. I was eventually moved from Logistics Plans officer to the Brigade Current Operations Chief (CUOPS). This position allowed me not to be TDY so much and to focus on writing and distributing orders and other actions throughout the brigade.

In February 2015, just before Valentine's Day, Jonathan and I discovered we were having a boy! We were so happy! We knew that he would be named Jonathan Montrace Van II. He would be the second of his name, the first of his kind! He would indeed be a prince! Then, one day, the wait was over! On June 19, 2015, Jonathan Montrace Van II was born! He was so precious. Jonathan kissed me and told me he was so proud of me. Then, he gave J2 his first bath. The next day, we celebrated Father's Day, and oh, what a gift! Our families came to see our new bundle of joy. J2 was welcomed into love and affection. He hollered the whole time! Lol Kidding! But he did eat the whole time! I guess it's true what they say: good things come to those who wait.

16

The Best Year of Your Life

In the winter of 2015, I competed in my primary zone for major. I spent time recovering from having a cesarian with J2 in order to be able to take an updated Army Physical Fitness test for my board. I got everything done and submitted it on time, along with my officer evaluation report. I was twenty-two years old when I had Ariel, and I recovered with no problem. I was thirty-two years old when I had J2. Recovering took on a whole new process. Although I had passed my PT Test and my height and weight, I was beginning to have more health problems. My knees, lower back, and feet were always aching and swelling.

Like every other soldier, I ignored my issues, took pain meds, and kept moving. I began to get depressed a lot and did not understand why. I was going through post-partum depression. An NCO advised me to go to pregnancy pt and train back up the right way, so I did. Being around the other women helped me to cope with the aftereffects of giving birth. I began to feel better about myself and got back to being a better mother and wife to my family. Often, it is hard for people who think everyone else wants them to be strong to fathom the thought of not being strong. That was me. I never wanted anyone to know how fragile I really was. Depression caused me to go into deep thought, and I would just write. I had friends, but those friends were not really happy or did not appear happy when I pulled away from everyone. But I needed time to take care of myself, which I rarely ever did. I was always so worried about helping other people that I was not present in the moments I needed to be with my family the most. So, through prayer, self-reflection, and talking to Jonathan, I got where I needed to be mentally, physically, emotionally, and spiritually.

I was doing well as the Current Operations Chief (CHOPS). It was a sunny day when the board results were released for major. I called Jonathan immediately! We were on the list! Yes, we (Jonathan, Me, Ariel, Jya, and J2). Not only had I married and changed my name to Captain Van, which is not how my Army legacy started, but when I tell you my Army legacy took off after I became Captain Van, it did just that! Now I was promotable and soon-to-be Major Van! A few days later, the list came out to tell us where we would attend school. We were on the list for Fort Leavenworth, Kansas. Yep, see ya later, Fort Knox! We are heading to Kansas! Nothing else could go wrong at that point. Everything was set, and then I began to have a bad pain in my side. I collapsed. My co-workers called Jonathan, and he met me at the hospital.

The nurse checked me and my vitals and told me that I was pregnant! At first, I was in shock. Jonathan and I were happy. But then she said, give us a day, and let's see what type of pregnancy it is. I immediately began to worry. Jonathan tried to keep me calm. That night, I had really bad pains to the point he rushed me back do the doctor. After checking my vitals and bloodwork, I was rushed back to surgery. I had an ectopic pregnancy, and the doctor explained that he took out my left fallopian tube to save me. I cried. Jonathan cried. We cried together. We were happy that we caught everything in time, but I was also sad that what would have been our second baby did not have a chance. This haunted me for a while. Every time I had another cycle, I cried. I cried for almost 6 months after this happened. It really hurt mentally.

Still in the healing process, we were all packed up and headed to Fort Leavenworth, Kansas. It was a different vibe than Fort Knox, and of course, it seemed to be in the middle of nowhere. With Leavenworth being the "First City" of Kansas, we did what we always did once we got somewhere new: we toured the happening spots. Looking at the surrounding areas, we decided to stay on post for the one year we were there for school. Everywhere we went, we were told that this would be the best year of our lives! I was almost done with all of my course work for my PhD and was getting to the point where I would meet my Chair and begin working on my prospectus. People thought it was crazy to work on a degree while attending the Command and General Staff College (CGSC), but I viewed it as a hobby away from the reality of attending classes all day. Working on my PhD allowed me time to decompress and focus on issues I cared about instead of trying to wrap my head around all the other courses we had to take at Leavenworth.

Just like any other military school, I was quiet, but I liked my small group. I thought we had a good mix of personalities, wisdom, egos, and backgrounds in our small group. We were only required to do one small group social, but we ended up having a few while we were there. I think it is important to form bonds and get to know people you work with outside of work. One of the things leaders mess up the most is not knowing their people. Regardless of rank, some social events need to happen so that your subordinates and peers can see you in a different setting. At the end of the day, we are all human. Nobody likes a stick in the mud. You have to be able to talk and relate to people. You do not have to like everyone, but you do have to respect them. I learned this throughout my career but exercised it a lot at Leavenworth.

My social outings at Leavenworth were very few. It had to be some-one's birthday or when my sorority sisters and I went to events. Other than that, I spent time with my family, Ariel's basketball games and track meets, and working on my prospectus. Once a few of the other wives and I got together, and we just all happened to be AKAs, we created friendships that are still alive and well to this day! They and their husbands and mine are all really good friends. We understood each other, and we respected our family time and each other's space.

The Command and General Staff College forced me to face my fears. It made me work harder in the areas that I was weak in. I wanted to be a better logistician and a better leader. I knew that leaving CGSC meant that I would be second in command in a battalion. I did not take this lightly. In fact, I worked up my nerves so badly that when Branch (HRC) came to talk to me, I told them I did not mind waiting to go into a key development position. Inside, I was not sure if I was ready. I had not psyched myself up to the challenge yet. Seriously, was I ready? I hated doubting myself, but I was going back and forth with myself about what I could do and not do. Jonathan came out of nowhere as if he had heard me thinking out loud. He asked me, "Why do you think you are not ready?" In true 'Mia Fashion,' I looked at him and said, "I don't know," and I honestly did not know. I told him that I wanted us to go overseas. I had not had an overseas assignment in my career, and why not do it with my family for the first time?

Jonathan was down! He was always ready for an adventure. So when I spoke back to Branch, I asked for Korea. No one else was trying to go to Korea. Sound familiar? So I confirmed that the assignment would be an "accompanied tour," and Branch said that it would be. I spoke to my friend, sister, and Soror, Dr. Margie Grines, who loved Korea, and she convinced me! So there you have it! I graduated from the Command and General Staff College received the Theater Sustainment Planner (P1) Identifier, and prepared our family to conduct our third permanent change of station from Fort Leavenworth, Kansas, to Daegu, South Korea.

17

Fight Tonight

Before flying to South Korea, we drove our Tahoe back to Mississippi. During that time, we spent time with our family and friends. We were excited as a family to go overseas. The elephant in the room was: will Jya be able to go? Being a single mother for almost nine years before getting married, I would have had several questions as well. So I sat down with Jya's mom and talked to her about South Korea and the opportunities that Jya had. She had to approve for Jya to go so that her and Jonathan could go together to get Jya's passport since she was a minor. So she did, and we were all set for South Korea. It took us approximately thirteen hours to fly from Seattle, Washington, to Seoul, South Korea. At the time, Dragon Hill Lodge and processing at Yongsan was the place to integrate into Korea. Then, a few days later, we were bused down to Daegu, South Korea.

We stayed at the Novotel in downtown Daegu while we waited for housing. Since we were a family of five, we ended up staying off-post. Staying off-post was amazing. We were able to experience the culture in a different way. We were immersed in it. The girls learned how to use taxis and their WAZE app to get around. They also learned how to use the subway. J2 attended a Korean Pre-K program. Jonathan volunteered with the football team, and I went straight to work as a Battle Major in the G3. The guy I was taking over from was very good at his job, and it was a smooth handover. My NCO and I got there almost a month after each other, and my new boss also came in. We entered Korea during a time of high tensions between South Korea, North Korea, and the United States. We ensured that we talked to our kids about what to do and where to meet if something ever happened. It sounds like something off of the movies, but we practiced this so if the time came to evacuate; we ensured everyone had a bag packed just in case. In Korea, we saw our kids blossom into full-blown butterflies. They were amazing and independent. J2 was still J2, but the girls were becoming young ladies.

As the Battle Major, I reviewed operations orders and prepared for an upcoming exercise when my boss, a full bird Colonel, called me to her office. I knew something was wrong because I don't get called to anyone's office. My boss was an African-American West Point Graduate from Alabama. She was not married and had no children. The first thing she did was ask me how I was doing. I answered, and then she proceeded to explain why she had called me in her office. She explained that our Commanding General received a call that I had kidnapped my 'stepdaughter,' her words, not mine. I never called Jya my stepdaughter; she is my daughter. I was taken aback, as some would say. Where did this even come from? So you mean to tell me Jya's mom called my Commanding General by herself with these accusations? Wow! This was lower than low. I sat down with her and explained everything. Why would she do this? I even told her I would send her money if she needed anything while Jya was gone. Was that my obligation? No, not really, but I was willing to help. In fact, I always was. When she did this, my heart turned cold. How dare you!? Why would you? Clearly, you do not care about anyone but yourself. This is where that phrase comes from, "Hurting people, hurt people," and that was her. What was reassuring to me was that I was new to the unit. My Commanding General only saw me in action a few times during our briefings with him. He told my boss that it did not sound like "Me" at all and to get to the bottom of it. So she called me in.

My boss wanted me to send Jya back. I told her that I was not. Jya wanted to be here, and her mother signed her passport paperwork for her to come. Jya was withdrawn from school and everything so that she could attend school in South Korea. Jonathan is her other parent, and he also has the right to care for her as he always has. For anyone who does not know, Jya is and always has been a daddy's girl. She and Jonathan have a bond out of this world. It is beautiful, and more fathers should follow suit. Anyway, no leader can legally tell a Soldier what to do in family matters. I learned this the hard way as a Company Commander. So, being on the receiving end, I did what all good Soldiers would do. I went to talk to legal. Legally, both parties signed the passport paperwork, thus consenting for Jya to be in her dad's care. So there, pound sand, and no, I'm not a kidnapper!

I felt a badge of shame initially when all of this happened. The only thing you have in this world is your name. You have to protect and defend your name like your life depends on it. I had no idea what people were saying about me or our family name. I knew in my heart that all intentions were always good in moving our entire family to South Korea to experience another culture together. No one was trying to break up anyone else's family. But do not throw rocks and then hide your hand, either. There are so many things that Jya underwent back home in Mississippi; which is her story to tell, but just know that what she went through back home is the reason she is shining bright like a diamond today. You cannot keep a good person down. Jya Van is a good person.

I continued to work and perform well at all my tasks as the Battle Major. I couldn't let my personal life or murmurs affect the job that I had come to Korea to do. My team and I performed well in our first exercise. Most of us were new and we learned a lot about what we could improve for next time. I am always about working smarter and not harder. I listen to my team when they make suggestions. We were recognized at the end of the exercise. My team received awards. I received the Commanding General's coin of excellence. Little did he know, earning that particular coin reassured me that I was still engaged, present for duty, and performing well.

Time went by fast, and before I knew it, the 19th Expeditionary Sustainment Command had published its slate for field grade officers. I was selected as the 25th Transportation Battalion's Operations Officer (S3). I was excited about this opportunity. Jonathan and I had recently gone to their Military Ball. I liked the morale of the unit. I was ready to get onboard and become a part of their team. However, before I left the G3, my boss did my senior rating counseling to close out my officer evaluation report. She was the second officer in my career who had really sat me down and talked about my performance and what I wanted to do next. Again, the first time I was a Company Commander talking to my battalion commander. This time, I was a Major. This was a rewarding experience, just to be told how you're doing and where you stand amongst your peers. Nothing about my evaluation surprised me when I received it for my signature. She set a new standard for me, and I appreciated that.

18

Consider It Done

As the Battle Major in the 19th ESC, my team and I received and processed all Serious Incident Reports (SIRs). I won't go into detail, but one particular SIR involved the 25th Transportation Battalion leaders. By the time I out-processed the 19th ESC and began to in-process at the 25th Transportation Battalion, the battalion had new leadership. I was informed that instead of being the Battalion S3, I would now be the Battalion XO. It was a weird time in the battalion as old members were leaving Korea and new members were coming. I took the opportunity to learn everything I could from JT and Kyle before they left the battalion. At least Kyle would be the Brigade XO in the Materiel Support Command-Korea (MSC-K).

One of the things I reflected on the most when I showed up to 25th is that I had my sights set on being the Battalion S3. I would have been comfortable in that seat since I was coming from being the 19th ESC G3, Battle Major. The S3 job is about synchronizing efforts, managing output and input, supporting the commander(s), and creating effective systems. I live for that stuff! Then I entered the building and was given the news of being the Battalion XO. My heart sank immediately. I did not think I was ready for that job at all. I wanted to believe that I was, but I was rusty on some things I needed to be sharp on as a Battalion XO. So I leaned head first on my staff. They, of course, were the experts in their areas, and we had sit-downs often to ensure we were good to go an all things: S1, S6, S4, Legal, and the Chaplain. It was a daunting task. At the same time that I was learning all of this in flight, I was also responsible for integrating our new Battalion Commander (BC) and his family.

The BC and his family were easy. He didn't require a whole lot of extra stuff. He was easy to talk to, and honestly, I felt like between the two of us and our new Command Sergeant Major, we were all figuring it out a few days at a time once they all got on board. Our Battalion S3 came on board, and she had been to Korea before and was also a good asset to the team. We called ourselves the Big 4 (BC, CSM, XO, S3). One of the first things the BC did was stop the staff from doing separate physical training from the Headquarters and Headquarters Detachment (HHD). People were upset! But I thought it was a good thing. Why not do pt with your Soldiers and support the HHD Commander and First Sergeant (1SG)? Now, for the record, I did not really care about running every day; especially over hilly terrain due to trouble with my knees and my feet, but I did it because the soldiers motivated me. It always felt good to run and do things with the soldiers. Truth be told, the Big four were all old and not too far apart in age. So it always smelled like Bengay or Icy Hot in the back of the formation! The S3 was in great shape. She would run to Yongsan and back if she could. We had a great team and worked well together.

One of my favorite parts of being the Battalion XO was walking around the battalion. Instead of always emailing my staff, I would go to their offices to talk with them. There were times when they came and sat in mine as well. I had a few chairs in my office, but the one everyone liked the most was the one right by the door. If they came in and closed the door after them, it would be something I would need to take action on. Overall, my staff was great. They were bright-eyed and bushy-tailed! I had the honor of working with two Chaplains during my time in the battalion. Both were assets to the battalion. They helped me a lot without even knowing it. They were vital in the success of the battalion. Our soldiers engaged with our Chaplains a lot, and the Chaplains were everywhere we were. Most commanders don't value Chaplains the way they should. Chaplains are your additional set of eyes and ears on the ground. They will keep you informed of the unit's morale and give you ideas on how to use different colors of money and resources to provide spiritual fitness for the soldiers and their families.

By the time an officer becomes a Battalion XO, most of the time, they have had more experience than their subordinates. When this is the case, you must balance what you know and be patient with their learning. Instead of giving answers, empower them to find the answer. Instead of fixing their problems, allow them to make mistakes and problem-solve to fix their own problems. Let your staff be independent while you oversee the communication and crosstalk amongst them. One thing I never liked was a staff member's "outing" someone in a meeting. The staff works for the Company Commanders and 1SGs. The staff is there for the command teams to be successful. Yes, the staff has several relationships and responsibilities that they must manage, but their overall goal should be for the command teams to be successful. If the command teams are unsuccessful, the staff is not doing their job. If you ever wanted me to go "Keesha" on you, throw someone under the bus in a meeting. As soon as the BC and CSM did closing remarks, I would say, "Staff, Standby." Not being a team player would get you dismissed from my presence with quickness. You better have faked it until you made it! But honestly, we did not have any spotlight rangers. Once we shared an understanding with the command teams and the staff, we were able to work together without ridiculous issues or spats.

There were times when I felt extremely overwhelmed and overworked.

I was constantly drained. I was not making it home in time to eat dinner with my family, which was the highlight of my day because I got to hear from them and check on their day. I spent too many late nights trying to catch up on work and check others' work. I would get to work early in the morning to work for a few hours before everyone came in. Then I would sometimes stay at work close to 8pm so as not to leave too much lingering for the next day. My body began to break down. I began to have long headaches that later turned into migraines. I did not sleep well at night. I was always on edge and constantly worried. I was becoming a shell of myself. I had several mental breakdowns that only Jonathan and I knew about. He was always there to catch me and speak life back into me. I was ready to give up almost weekly. My feelings were getting more and more fragile dealing with people in general. I did not afford myself any grace. I was exhausted. I felt like I was alone and no one understood. But on the outside, I smiled, joked with people, and performed like I had superpowers. But I hid depression, anxiety, and worry so well within. Finally, I went to behavioral health to talk to someone. I felt silly being there at first because the counselor went down my list of accomplishments. She did it in a way as to ask me why I was feeling sorry for myself. Why did I feel like I was not worthy? I had already broken through generational curses and other stereotypical barriers. Why did I not feel good about myself? The counselor had me write a letter to my younger self to tell my younger self everything that I needed to know and that I had learned in my adult life. For three days, I sat and thought about what I wanted to tell my younger self. This was the most difficult task I had been asked to do. By the time I completed the letter, it was about ten pages.

My BC never counseled me. I assumed it was because we talked about everything every day. I covered for him when he was on vacation. I literally ran the battalion behind the scenes. I did not seek or want the spotlight. I was ok doing what I needed to do. The awkwardness came in when I sat down with my Brigade Commander for my initial counseling and my final senior rater counseling before becoming the Battalion XO. He spoke a lot about himself and the sacrifices he made. One of the things that stood out to me the most was when he told me, "In order to be the best, you have to beat the best." I will never forget those words. I had to do some soul-searching. He had me questioning myself. Was I doing a good job as the Battalion XO? Do I really need to outscore everyone else on my PT Test? I need surgery, but maybe I should hold off on that and just soldier on. I had so many things going through my mind. I left my final counseling with him, not knowing where I stood amongst my peers. It was a bad feeling. When I saw my officer evaluation report, my BC had me as 2 of 2 Majors that he currently rates. After everything that I endured to make sure that the battalion was successful? I put myself on the back burner, and I am second in command of you. Did he really rate me as the second best? Wow! That was a hard blow for me. No explanation, no this is my reasoning, nothing. Crickets.

Then the Brigade Commander rated me as the number four major he senior rated. How could I be mad? My own BC rated me as second, so of course, I knew the S3 got a better rating than me from both. The one thing I did not understand was how and why. So, instead of being mad about it, I was already positioning to move over and take the S3 position. I did not really do a hand over with the S3, and I didn't really need to. I did not like how the shop was run. It was my forte, and I knew I was ready to do it better.

As I transitioned from the Battalion XO to the Battalion S3, our S3 left to go to Brigade. We had a new Brigade Commander, and he actually came from the 19th ESC Staff. I helped onboard a new Battalion XO that was coming from Camp Humphreys. She was very quiet and came right as COVID-19 began to sweep South Korea. So, I operated as the X3 (XO and S3) for a short time. When our Brigade Headquarters went down due to everyone being sick from COVID-19, our battalion was chosen to cover down, attend all briefings, and provide reports for the rest of the brigade. I had a great team in the S3. They were mostly new personnel, and some had been there since I was the XO.

We all worked well together. We quickly reached out to the other Battalion XOs/S3s to get them onboard with how we were receiving reports, compiling them, and actively tracking 24-hour operations due to COVID-19. My Battle Captains were broken up into two shifts at first, and then we began to overlap into three shifts, with me floating due to meetings. I was never told why our battalion was chosen to spearhead the efforts when the brigade went down, but I know that when the brigade came back up, we gave it back to them better than they gave it to us. We streamlined systems. We fixed communications with each battalion. Of course, our BC was set up for success during his briefings. At one point, we ran one or two of the Brigade's meetings as they came back on board. Within almost a week, our small battalion ran an entire brigade's worth of personnel and did not complain, whine, or say it was not our job, but we did what needed to be done. Hence, our battalion motto was, "Consider It Done!"

During COVID-19, things were difficult in our home. Jonathan did not want me putting myself or our family in harm's way as I went to work each day. We wore masks and gloves, but it was still a chance each day I had to go to work. Jonathan and I overcame an issue that had been weighing heavily on our family and constantly being held over my head by my BC, but God! God worked it all out. I continued to work on my prospectus and got it approved. I also completed a Master's Degree in Philosophy while working toward completing my prospectus. Jonathan coached the Daegu High School Girls Basketball Team, and they were headed to win their second Championship, but COVID-19 happened, and they returned to Korea to quarantine. In the meantime, I was in touch with my branch manager, who was one of my fraternity brothers and a good friend. He told me about the opportunity of being an Aide-de-camp and about being an instructor at the United States Military Academy. I pondered about both but felt that teaching would be more rewarding. He hooked me up with the specifics of applying to the Army Civil Schooling Program through the United States Military Academy, and I was called for a phone interview. The rest was history! We got an Exception to Policy to leave Korea under COVID-19 constraints, and it was granted. We were headed back to the United States!

19

Duty, Honor, Country

My family and I arrived in the United States when COVID-19 was still new to its population. We hadn't seen our family in three years and decided to stay with my parents during our leave time before heading to New York. It was a weird time in the world. Some people believed COVID-19 was real, some didn't. Since we came from Korea, we had plenty of masks, and we wore them actively. We were caught off guard when COVID-19 hit Korea, but Korea quickly figured out how to operate with it until things were resolved. The United States was different. We quarantined about as much as we could stand with everyone in one house all day for several days. Because of COVID-19, we only got to see immediate family. In Mississippi, people were still out and about like nothing had happened. Some wore masks, some didn't. If we had to go anywhere, we wore our masks and kept Clorox wipes.

As our time in Mississippi came to an end, one day, my mama found a painting that Ariel drew during our stay and showed it to me. Ariel had always been the artist in our family. She used art to express herself, and she was good at it. This particular painting expressed thoughts of not wanting to be around anymore, pictures of no one caring, helpless and hopeless thoughts, and then anger. I vaguely remember each detail drawn on the canvas, but I remember how I felt when I saw the painting. My heart sank. I immediately went to talk to Ariel. It was at that moment that she expressed how she had been feeling. She had been cutting herself, and she was having suicidal ideations. She wrote a letter to me asking me to help her. She showed me the letter after I found out about the painting. I read her letter and cried. She wanted me to help her. "You help everyone else; well, I need you to help me." I quickly researched the suicide hotline number. I called them, and a counselor came to our home within an hour. She spoke to Jonathan and me with Ariel, and then she spoke to Ariel alone. Afterward, it was determined that Ariel needed to go to the Children's Behavioral Health Center in South Jackson. We were three days away from leaving to go to New York and sign in. We were in the process of packing the U-haul and washing clothes to get ready to go. Initially, the plan was not to take Deuce with us; we would relook picking him up later once we figured out the housing plan in New York. Instead, all our plans took a detour because our daughter's health was more important than rushing off to a new duty station. Remembering what happened to me the last time I took a family matter into my own hands, I informed the unit that I would be a little delayed in arriving. Due to COVID-19, so many things were backed up, and the unit was ok with us taking as much time as needed.

Ariel was in care for almost two weeks. We took turns going to see her. Because of COVID-19, we were limited on who could visit and how often we could visit. There were so many speculations about what could have made her feel like she did not need to be alive. It hurt just thinking about it, but we all knew that she was in the best place for care. She was placed on light meds, heavily monitored, and was able to interact with other teen girls who were in the center as well. Each day we visited her, she wanted to know when she was coming home. We always replied, "When you get better, the medical staff will inform us that you can go. Just keep working on expressing yourself and getting better." I cried internally each time we were there, and when we got back in the car, I bawled each time. It was so hard to see my baby girl go through something like this. As a mother, I felt like I had failed her. What was I missing? Did something happen to her? What was she not telling me? For a while, I was mad at the girl that Ariel said she was dating before we left Korea. But then I realized Ariel was smart enough to make her own decisions. I just prayed that she would cooperate with the doctors and care team so that she could be released to come home.

One of the things I admire about Ariel is that she has always been strong. I admired the fact that she had taken on so much that she was able to say, "Hey, I am not strong enough to deal with some of these feelings that I am having; I need some help." This was big and very important for her journey as a teenager and soon to be a young adult. Ariel cautioned all of us to stop and think. We all had to take a step back and look outside of ourselves in order to provide the best support system she needed to get through this. After a few more evaluations, Ariel was assigned meds to take, and we was released to travel to New York, but we had to enroll her in continued care with a counselor upon arrival. Due to COVID-19, it was hard to choose a counselor ahead of time, so that would be one of the first things we would do once we checked into a hotel. Deuce, our Boxer, was also registered to be Ariel's emotional support animal, and he too joined us on the ride up to New York.

As we began driving from Mississippi to New York, we were leaving as a new family. We were now a family that had experienced something that we never saw coming. It made us more resilient and more aware of each other's needs and vulnerabilities. It took us two days to get to New York. We only stayed at hotels that were pet-friendly. Deuce was still crazy, though! He barked at everyone he saw. He had no chill. During bathroom breaks, Ariel walked him and fed him. Deuce was a handful. But he had Ariel, and Ariel had him.

We drove with a U-haul trailer on the back of our Tahoe. We made it from Jackson, Mississippi, to the bridge crossing into Delaware when the U-haul trailer came unhitched as I was driving down the bridge. I saw the trailer swaying in my rearview mirror. I tried not to panic as Jonathan talked me through getting the truck and trailer pulled over out of traffic without us or it flipping over or causing a wreck. Other cars went around us. I slowly tapped the breaks as to try to slow the trailer down. The trailer was yanking and pulling away from the truck but never slammed into the back of it as we continued down the hill. Once we made it off of the bridge and slowly pulled onto the shoulder of the interstate, I let out a gasp of air and cried and hyperventilated hysterically. It was nothing but God that kept us all in that moment. That could have been much worse than what had happened; thank you, God, for traveling grace! A police officer pulled over to assist us. Jonathan told him what happened. We realized that one pin was not hooked in. Of course, it was the safety pin that was missing. Jonathan unhooked the trailer, and we drove Tahoe (which had no damage at all, nor did the trailer) to the nearest Auto Zone to get the missing pin. It added 45 minutes to our trip, and we got the U-haul hooked back up correctly and continued towards New York City.

We felt a sigh of relief once we crossed the New York state line. We knew we were close to West Point and our hotel, where we would reside off-post. Because of COVID-19, traffic was not too bad. Not a lot of people were on the roads. Once we made it to our hotel, we were relieved, tired, happy, anxious, and thankful. We rested that night. The next day, we took a short journey to The United States Military Academy (West Point). It was truly beautiful! Historic buildings, mountains, old homes, and, of course, the Hudson River. West Point was truly a sight to see. We all smiled in awe of our new journey. We realized that the Thayer Hotel on post did not seem to be full. Jonathan called and worked his magic as usual. We were able to move from the hotel in Fort Montgomery to the Thayer Hotel until a house was ready on post.

Due to COVID-19, several systems and processes didn't happen right away. Everyone was teleworking. Housing was teleworking. We made it to West Point in June. We did not move into our house until August. I feel like the housing office was not truthful at all about its inventory. West Point, like most military installations, has housing set aside by rank. However, this was not entirely the case at West Point. West Point was totally different from anywhere we'd been in the military. As a field grade officer, I outranked everyone on my street. Some people who did not outrank me had newer homes, had bigger homes, and lived in a neighborhood equivalent to my rank. I guess housing was just bombarded due to COVID-19 because they just sprinkled us all in. Rank immaterial! Housing gave us a home choice to view.

I made it very clear to them that I needed a fence because I had our dog. They told me I needed to build one, and I would have to get approval. So when they recommended the house on Merritt Road, when we went to view it (without housing due to COVID-19), the house had a wooden fence that was the correct height per the Grey Ghost neighborhood policy. When we signed our lease and were told our move-in date was in August, the fence was gone! I called housing. "What happened to the fence?" Housing agent, "It was taken down; you have to pay for and build your own fence." Me, "Why would you remove a fence that is already there? We only chose this house because it had the fence." Housing agent, "I apologize for any confusion. For this neighborhood, each resident has to build their own fence." Jonathan and I were on ten! After we moved in, Deuce, Ariel, J2, and Jya would walk to the dog park so Deuce could play. We realized that purchasing a $10,000 fence for two to three years made no sense if they were just going to cut it down like they did the one there before. That was our first West Point encounter.

In the meantime, as we waited for household goods and my car to arrive from Korea, we set up sessions by telephone for Ariel with a counselor. Her calls were weekly as she began to get settled in. When we were staying at Thayer, the counselor was able to see her in person a few times. Ariel seemed to be doing better. We kept a close eye on her. In fact, we kept a close eye on each other. COVID-19 brought about different dilemmas, and the fact that we had done COVID-19 in Korea and Mississippi, COVID-19 was still being done differently in New York. The kids were all registered for school, and their sports physicals were complete, but no sports were happening due to COVID-19. They had gone from being about to operate in COVID-19 to not operating at all. It was hard on everyone. By the time school began in New York, it was all virtual for the girls, as they were in their Junior year of high school.

J2 was virtual initially; he attended kindergarten at West Point Elementary. Later in the year, West Point opened back up with a choice for J2 to attend in person or online. You better believe we sent him to school with his mask! School for J2 online was super hard. How in the world do you expect five-year-olds to focus online if it's not spiderman or Pokémon? For the girls, it was even more challenging. They were missing the human connection, the social life, and the break away from the house. They were not able to get jobs until everything opened up again. Their Junior year was tough on them.

As for me, my job for the first year stationed at West Point was to attend Columbia Teacher's College and obtain a Higher Post Secondary Education Masters. To do this, I put my PhD on hold and got down to business. Once again, due to COVID-19, our cohort did not travel back and forth to the city or live in the city. All of our classes were online. Before graduation, I had one more final project to complete. It was a group project. Our group had been working on the project since February, and it was due in April. It was March 2, 2021, that I received a hysterical call from my mom that my dad had collapsed on the living room floor at their home. I put her on speaker so Jonathan could hear as well. I asked her did she call 911. Was the ambulance on the way? She said she did. A neighbor from across the street was a nurse and rushed over to help my mom with my dad. He was unresponsive. The ambulance finally made it there and began to work on dad. He was still unresponsive. My mom was very hysterical, and I felt helpless because there was no way to calm her down. We tried to talk to her as calmly as we could. I did not think of anything or anyone else in those moments. I only thought about my dad. Was he going to be ok? How long had he been unresponsive? What did he eat that night? He wasn't sick, did he possibly have COVID-19? No, he didn't have COVID-19. I had so many questions.

The ambulance rushed my dad to the hospital. I immediately began working flights to get us home. This was a state of emergency as far as I was concerned. I notified my unit. I called Morgan Farms and told the lady what was happening. She was able to board Deuce for us while we flew to Mississippi. We made it to Mississippi on March 4th. It felt like the next day, but it wasn't due to dropping Deuce off and getting ourselves together. The girls were still going to school online, so we pulled J2 out temporarily to travel. We immediately rushed over to drop the kids and bags off, and then we went to the hospital.

Because of COVID-19, only people on the list in the hospital and immediate family could go and see my dad. By this time, daddy was in the ICU. Jonathan and I felt like my mom was leaving some things out over the phone. I'm sure that with everything going on, she was juggling a lot. I was able to go up to the ICU and see my dad. My mom and Bugg were already in there. The nurse allowed me to come in. Based on what the nurse said and what the doctor said, as I looked at my dad and talked to him in that hospital, I knew on March 4th that he was ready to go. Maybe he was fighting, or perhaps he just wanted to go the way he wanted to, which was in his chair at his home. I rubbed his feet and talked to him. I held his hand. I kissed him and told him I love him and that I understand. When I walked out of the hospital that day, I knew that I had a huge task in front of me. Daddy had said goodbye, but now it was time for everyone else to. I sat in the car and cried until I could not cry anymore. I was devasted. Amidst how I was feeling, I checked on my mom and asked if she had called dad's side of the family or hers. She had not. She had a million reasons why she didn't, and I tried to explain to her that letting everyone know what was going on was the right thing to do. I tried to keep her calm but also keep my family informed. It was like World War III, but only one person was fighting; everyone else was grieving and concerned.

With a great task at hand, I began calling my siblings, aunts, and uncles. I informed family from both sides. One of my siblings I could not locate until right up to the week of the funeral, and she still did not come, but that's ok. She was informed about everything happening with dad. I understood that my mom was hurting. I understood that she was the only one with the authority to make decisions concerning my dad. I tried to always be her voice of reason, but she was in pain and had to deal with things the best way she knew how. It left the rest of us hurting and in despair. My mom kept my dad in the ICU until he had to be moved to another hospital and basically waited for him to either wake up or go on to heaven. By the time she made that decision, my dad's side of the family had come from Chicago to see him. My oldest brother and sister-in-law also made it on time to see dad in the new location. After that, my family and I had to fly back to New York. We had to get Deuce out of boarding and regroup for a moment. Emotions were high, times were tough, and we were all carrying the burden of sadness and despair.

I could not sleep being back in New York. I called my mom daily to check on my dad. Jonathan comforted me and always encouraged me through it all. He was a godsend. He had lost his mother, Ms. Vanessa, when he was a senior in high school, and nine years later, he lost his sister, Veronica. Looking at Jonathan and Veronica side by side, they could've easily been twins! Everyone who knew Ms. Vanessa agreed that Jya looked just like her! Jonathan helped me to prepare for what was indeed coming. You don't really see people's true colors until you lose a loved one.

On April 21, 2021, Jonathan got a call from mom that my dad had passed away. My phone did not ring, or maybe it did. But I did not hear it. I was super numb. At that moment, I felt relieved. I was glad that daddy was finally able to rest. My mom, of course, was upset and distraught. She tried to have his funeral two days later. My cousin called me with this news because she was there helping my mom after she got the call. She had talked my mom into waiting until we got back to Mississippi. Being in New York, I knew my family had the farthest to go. We spent a lot flying home in March when things first happened. We had just flown back and been back about a week. Jonathan and I decided that driving would be the more cost-effective way, and we could take Deuce with us and leave him there for moral support. It felt like we drove through the night, but we did stop and rest halfway through the trip down to Mississippi.

Everyone who could make it out during COVID-19 times saw my dad off. My mom didn't want anything to do with anyone. I had no idea why she was taking everything so personally. I did not get it until I talked to a Behavioral Health Therapist when I returned to New York. I realized that it was my mom's way of grieving. We all grieve in different ways. On April 26, 2021, we buried my dad. Before and after the funeral, my siblings and I reconnected and have been in touch since. I thank everyone who had a hand in buying flowers and helping with the repass, funeral arrangements, headstone, and obituary. March and April 2021 changed me forever. I will never be the same Mia that you met before that time.

I did not set foot on Columbia's campus until after graduation when New York was slowly opening up. In fact, our graduation was virtual, but my family took me to see the campus in person and to take a few cap and gown pictures at the college. J2 also completed kindergarten, so we decided to take pictures together to remember those accomplishments.

One way I dealt with grieving the loss of my dad was by going straight to work. I worked in the Department of Military Instruction (DMI) at the United States Military Academy (USMA). One of our department's most significant events was planning and executing Cadet Summer Training. I was familiar with how ROTC conducted summer training, but I knew that USMA would be different. The officer I was replacing was retiring, and I was able to do a good handover with him. When I met my senior rater for the first time, he expressed his condolences for the loss of my dad. I almost fell out in the Cadet Summer Training (CST) Tactical Operations Center (TOC), but God kept me on my feet. Instead, I truly appreciated his support and kind words. Thinking back on how senior leaders had treated me with family matters earlier in my career, here I was as a Major, and my senior rater, a Caucasian Colonel and West Point Graduate, who only knew me through my Officer Record Brief (ORB), that wanted me to come onboard, extended the proper respects. I could only wonder why I did not expect good things to happen to me. Why did I not think or feel worthy to be shown compassion? My emotions were all over the place, but I always appreciated him for that. It was a great introduction to DMI. I even conducted telephonic calls with my therapist in between meetings and lunch breaks while out at Camp Buckner as time allowed. This also helped me cope and be a more effective leader.

Cadet Summer Training (CST) 2021 was my trial-and-error summer with my new team. I learned a lot. I had the team create a Standard Operating Procedure (SOP) based on the lessons we learned and how we adjusted things in motion to provide effective sustainment throughout the summer. This was nerve-wracking but also fun for me. I enjoyed a good challenge and actively problem-solved with my team and the Details running each portion of summer training for their respective cadet classes. My rater during this time was a lieutenant colonel. He was super hyper and slightly annoying, but he did have our back when we needed it most.

The only thing I did not like about him was the comments he would make regarding rank. He would say things like, "You have to have some rank to get anything done here at West Point" or "Let him know because he goes direct with the people in charge." He would sometimes make references like that to me in front of my team. I did not appreciate it, but I never spoke up for myself. I just kept on working and making things happen. And for the record, I never needed rank to get anything done. I only went and talked to people face to face. It's easy to hide behind a computer at Camp Buckner, but it is much better to go in person where the friction seems to be. I spent that summer meeting all of the key players and getting their perspectives on how we can better prepare for next summer. Crazy enough, it worked. But what I will say is that my therapist gave me a few breathing techniques to implement when people like him struck a nerve, and she also had me record how I would feel in that moment and replay it later. I found this technique very interesting. Seeing yourself in an unstable and emotional state, calming down, and watching it later felt like Dr. Jekyll and Ms. Hyde! Seriously, was I losing my mind? Or did I just need to say what was on my mind? For a long time, even in my adult life, I felt that if I told people exactly what was on my mind, I would never have any friends, family, a man, or anything. I used to view people speaking their minds as assholes. But they are not. They are brave. But so am I. My therapist had me read a book called "The Power of Saying No," and it helped me to work through standing up for myself and not feeling guilty about not wanting to do something and letting someone else down. It was time for me to start doing more of what I wanted to do and stop being a people pleaser. Easier said than done!

After March Back, we had a week to reorganize and prepare for the academic school year. When we are not planning or executing CST, we are teaching Military Science and Training about hundred new cadets (Plebes). During this week, we also had to close out summer training.

My shop oversaw several contracts and coordinated a lot with the Department of Public Works (DPW) and the Logistics Readiness Center (LRC). Barracks were turned back over, weapons turned in, and the Task Force redeployed back to Fort Drum, NY. It was a busy time with a shop of three. The S4 shop consisted of me and my two NCOs. We did a lot of heavy lifting.

At least during the summer, we were augmented with newly promoted West Point 2nd Lieutenants. It was our time to groom them on officer and NCO relationships, staff work, and supply operations. Our lieutenants worked hard in the Sustainment Cell because, as you know, logistics is 24/7. Since it was my first semester teaching, I was a little nervous, anxious, and excited all at the same time. I wanted to make a good impression on the cadets. I had not seen many African American female officers around the academy, but they were spread out in different departments. In my department, I was the only one. I had gotten a chance to meet and work with many other officers in the department by way of CST. The department's first staff ride also provided a better glimpse into meeting other sections within DMI. Out of the other departments at USMA, I felt like our department was the best! It was military-minded, and we had officers and NCOs competing for promotions, other jobs, etc. We had a few who were retiring as well, and the department supported them as well. It was a good place to be. Definitely a hidden secret!

My first year as an instructor flew by. I went in nervous but quickly turned it into a therapy session for me and my cadets! Lol. We got through our material and key concepts, but we also had a good time. In the fall semester, we mostly wore masks due to COVID-19 concerns. Halfway through the semester, we stopped wearing masks. It all worked out ok. During the fall semester, my team and I also held planning meetings in preparation for Cadet Summer Training (CST) 2022. I quickly realized that each cell had been planning their training separately, but it was disjointed. Creating a centralized meeting for all sustainment coordination and synchronization helped all cell leads and detail planners to collaborate and discuss issues earlier on instead of during the actual summer training. I also linked in all of the outside agencies that supported the entire summer training, from the G4 to the MICC to the LRC and DPW. My shop worked with planners to forecast their requirements early, allowing us time to adjust and confirm contracts. We also worked with Cadet Mess to streamline meals and the entire summer's field feeding plan. It was a lot of moving pieces. We still graded papers, listened to briefs, conducted physical fitness, and spent time with our families. It was a busy time, but by spring, we were in full force with closing the semester and preparing to onboard the Task Force from Fort Campbell and set the theater for Cadet Summer Training 2022.

Before I get too far ahead of myself, I want to explain that in 2021, it was so hard on my family during my dad's passing, COVID-19 online schoolwork, and being teenagers. The girls had a rough year going to school online in New York. They only went to their school twice in person to pick up their Chromebooks and once for an attempt to go back with masks. They were missing the social side of being teenagers. Dating or going out with your friends was not happening during COVID-19. They had a BMW that they shared when they were working at Walgreens. A scary night happened, and they let their friend drive, who had a seizure while driving and wrecked the car, with them and their other friends in it! Thank God none of the kids were hurt that night. Of course, this happened when Jonathan, J2, and I went to Atlantic City for a getaway and left the girl's home. We were furious with them for not being more responsible but we could care less about them wrecking the car. They both had to pay the deductible for the insurance. Jonathan got them another car. This time, it was a little dune buggy. Then, one day at dinner, Jya made what she called a big announcement. She wanted to go back to Mississippi for her senior year. Jonathan and I were both shocked. So I asked Ariel if she was considering the same thing. She looked like she wanted to say not really, but she just said yes. To this day, I feel like I should've just not asked her. But things happen for a reason. So it was done. Both girls went back to live in Mississippi and graduated from Brandon and Callaway High Schools. Jya stayed with her mom. Ariel stayed with her dad.

I also spent time preparing myself to compete for lieutenant colonel. I also began working on my doctorate again, hoping to complete it before leaving and going to another duty station. So many things were happening around me. I was so overwhelmed. I was super emotional, and I was so fragile. I had to put on a facade of how and who I was so that I could continue to serve. Inside, I was depressed. I was mad and angry. I had such a heavy heart. I took everything that anyone said as a personal attack. I was getting mad at people who I thought were "coming for me"; some were, and some were not. The only thing that kept me sane was to keep working towards completing my doctorate and attending Sunday Chapel services. So I pressed on.

I competed for promotion to lieutenant colonel. The results came out as Jonathan, J2, and I were in Jamaica during Spring Break 2022! I was selected Merit-Based for Lieutenant Colonel! God is good! All the time! And all the time, God is good! Our spring break vacation turned into a celebration as we soaked up the beautiful Jamaican sun. What a blessing! Three other majors and I in our department made the lieutenant colonel list, but only two of us were merit-based. I decided to have my promotion ceremony after summer training and before the beginning of the semester. My family was so proud of me. Because of them, I always went so hard, and everything I did was for my family. My cousins from Texas flew in. Our friends from Fort Belvoir drove up. Ariel, Jya, and Bugg, along with friends from South Carolina and Texas, also flew in. It was a cool time to celebrate my success with loved ones and close friends.

I enjoyed being a Logistician. Problem-solving was my thing. It did not seem like work. It was a hobby and fun to do. Seeing the people you inspired along the way while mentoring and guiding them was all worth it to me. I wish I had a mentor early on in my career that looked like me and had my best interest in mind. One thing I will tell you is that it is hard to find genuine people. But they are out there. I am still in touch with people who are genuine and have my best interest in mind. We may not talk every day and possibly go months at a time, but when we do talk again, we pick right back up where we left off. Those are real friends. No judgment, no hard feelings, they love to see you win, you love to see them win, and they speak positively about you when you are not around to talk about yourself.

My team and I executed CST 22. It was a bit challenging, but we got through it more fluidly than we did the previous summer. Sometimes, a little success is better than no success at all. There were times during CST 22 when I would get into it with other Majors, but not many, only a few. Most of the time, they happened to be Infantry officers, but things eventually worked out. My intent was to never go back and forth with someone but to get to the bottom of the problem, solve it, and move on. No hard feelings. We do not have to like each other, but you will respect me and my team. One of my NCOs was planning to retire that summer. He gave us the last fight he had in himself, and we bid him farewell after that summer.

In the fall of 2022, I taught my next round of cadets. It was exciting, and I considered myself a natural after teaching the previous year. I stood before my new cadets as a Lieutenant Colonel. Teaching continued to be a rewarding experience. Halfway through the fall semester, I attended the Battalion Command Assessment Program (BCAP) at Fort Knox, KY. It differed from any type of Army training/classes I had ever attended. The Army was trying to get it right. It wanted good, genuine leaders who cared about people. The Army I grew up in had more toxic and counterproductive leaders than good ones. My generation of officers learned how to be and do better by getting mostly bad examples. It sounds bad, but it's true.

BCAP was geared to weed out the bad leaders and to keep the good ones. It was an interesting experience. I learned a lot about myself as a person, a wife, a mother, a leader, and most of all, as a Christian. My faith has guided me in my entire career. Even during the times when it seemed like I did not know Jesus at all, He was always with me. He forgave me. The only thing left was forgiving myself, picking my head up, and moving on. I had been humbled for too long. BCAP challenged me to look deeper inside what I saw on the surface each morning. I was good to other people and good for other people, but I was not being good to myself. I needed to extend myself some grace. That AHA moment took me through the roof at BCAP! I was now operating in a space of confidence, likeness, love, and grace. Looking back, I count it all joy!

In the spring of 2023, it was announced that I would take command of the Defense Logistics Agency Energy Battalion in South Korea! Oh my goodness, we were going back to Korea! We were super excited. 2023 was the year of news after news, all good news! As I began to spread my good news, I also successfully defended my dissertation and received confirmation from my committee that I was now Dr. Jeremia Van! I instantly began to inform my family members and close friends. My family was very supportive. I planned to walk the stage in Orlando, Florida, that July! Everything was aligned, and we met up with our family in Orlando. We had a great time exploring and preparing for graduation. I gifted each of my children and my husband a personalized manuscript of my dissertation with a message unique to each of them. They had kept me inspired the entire journey.

The summer of 2023 was super full for me and my team. It was an interesting summer, but not bad at all. The young man who arrived to replace me did not get to shadow me personally but took on the responsibilities of another detail to help out another officer. I was able to sit with him throughout the school year and leading up to Cadet Summer Training 2024 to help him get situated. As I began to prepare for battalion command, I quickly realized that I did not have much time to spend outside of traveling to four different training courses that all related to me taking command. My two outstanding NCOs helped cover my classes when I was absent. I taught most of my fall classes, but by the time spring came, I was in and out for training again, and when I came back, I had finally received my orders for Korea. I had to shift focus to get my family packed, my vehicle shipped, my house turned in, and hotels scheduled before leaving New York. Planning is what I do. I assess. I execute! I say I, but it was a team effort. We don't call ourselves Team Van for nothing. When we move, we move together with one voice. I love Jonathan with my mind, body, and soul. He is my person, mi amor. In the final chapter, I will explain more about Jonathan and how he contributed immensely to where I am now in my career, life, and my own little safe space.

20

A Higher Degree, A Higher Purpose

I had known my husband Jonathan for over ten years before we decided to actively date and later get married. He tells everyone that we met on Christian Mingle.com, but we met at our drill unit, the 894th Quartermaster Company, in Jackson, Mississippi. Jonathan had always been a comedian. He was always very confident. He looked good in his uniform, and his boots shined nicely. He cared about his appearance. It showed. When he was in civilian clothes, he also cared about his appearance. Jonathan is the type of man who knows what he wants and is not afraid to voice it or show it. On the other hand, I thought I knew what I wanted, and I thought I had life all figured out, but honestly, neither one of us did. We laugh about it in the present day as we reflect and remember that neither of us would have been good for each other when Jonathan tried to put his arm around me, and I moved it out of the way. I still do not remember moving his arm out of the way, or even if it happened, but he says it happened! Lol

It took God 10 years to mold me into who I needed to be for Jonathan and who Jonathan needed to be for me. We had no idea. I was tired of failed relationships, and those failed relationships always started the same. I just assumed it was me. One day, I discussed with my parents, who had been married for forty-plus years, that I kept running into roadblocks in my relationships. My parents explained to me that I should not be forcing anything. They said something like, "Don't feel like you must be with someone. You could be single and happy for the rest of your life if you wanted." That messed me up. I did not comment to them about it at the time, but those words haunted me. How could they say that to me? I would often think to myself. Why would they say that to me?

To this day, I have no clue why, and I don't think it was meant to be taken literally, but I love words. Words matter to me. I hang on to words and the context in which they are displayed or communicated verbally. The ironic part about that conversation is that a few years later, I began to be at peace with being by myself. I focused more on loving myself, actively loving God, and thanking him for everything he had done for me. It was then and only then that I was able to reconnect with Jonathan. One date at Chuck E. Cheese with the girls, and the rest was history!

After Jonathan and I got married on May 31, 2014, I knew then that I had only two more things that I wanted to accomplish. The first one was that we both wanted to have a child together. We were crazy about our daughters. We prayed and asked God for a son. I did not conceive easily, or at the time, that I thought we should have, considering our circumstances. To not focus so heavily on conceiving, I decided to focus on my second accomplishment. I wanted to obtain my PhD. Before searching for the right school to support all my needs as a mom, wife, and active duty Army officer, I asked Jonathan what he thought about the idea, and he fully supported me. He encouraged me and supported me in ways I never knew I needed. After researching several different schools, I decided on Walden University. Their motto was "A Higher Degree, A Higher Purpose." Walden University supports the military community, and most of all, it supports adults who work full-time. Walden is focused on supporting positive social change throughout the world. A degree with Walden could be obtained online and with multiple face-to-face audiences, including professors, committees, study partners, colleagues, and veteran support. I made my choice. In 2014, I began taking classes towards my doctoral degree.

Many people were confused about how and why I was working on my PhD. Discussing my goals with other people made them want to question me even more or offer feedback and opinions that I did not ask for. The old me let them say what they wanted to say, whether it hurt my feelings or not, and I never truly stood up for myself. The new me will not stand for any foolish comments. Either come to me correct or don't come at all. I no longer go along with what others say to spare their feelings. The reality is that you can't share your dreams, goals, and ambitions with everyone. Everyone will not believe in you the way you believe in yourself. People say one thing in front of you and then say something totally different behind your back. Make sure that whatever you decide to do in life, you do it for yourself and your family. Keep only the people who have shown you through their actions that they truly love, care, and are rooting for you to win. These are the same people who are ok with you shining even when they are not. These are the same people that you always root for to win, and when they win, you are happy for them, even if you have not hit your winning season. These people are rare, but they are out there.

My journey at Walden began with me taking one course a quarter. I completed my assignments and group discussions at night. I went to a total of four Residencies in order to meet other colleagues in my discipline. I worked on my course load classes from 2014 to 2016. From 2016 to 2019, I worked on my prospectus, and I finally completed it. I completed my master's in philosophy in 2018 while working toward my PhD. I chose to study Philosophy and Management with a concentration in Leadership and Organizational Change. The organization I planned to focus on was the one I spent most of my life in, the Army. I noticed throughout my career that women seemed to be few and few, depending on what type of unit you were in. I did not see a lot of African American female officers as I came up in the ranks. When I finally did, I was literally a Major. That's ten years since I was commissioned as a second lieutenant. One thing that I noticed was that women battled with different issues than men when serving on active duty. Whether the women were married, single, or dual military, other challenges always seemed to weigh in on whether they would continue to serve. This is still a problem.

Women have made leaps and bounds in the military, but how often do you see successful women who are still serving? How many women do you see that look like you? Every soldier has a story to tell. The connection with women, their service to their country, and their personal stories led me to my dissertation topic, "Career Progression: Narrative Study of Impediments Affecting Army Female Officer Advancement from Major to Lieutenant Colonel."

In choosing a Dissertation Chair, I initially chose a Caucasian male. He and I fought back and forth on my initial topic, "Career Progression of African American Women in the Military." He was sure that research on this topic had already been done and that I would not be adding to a body of work or discipline. I chose another Dissertation Chair six months later. This Chair was an African American woman who challenged me not to start with a title for my research but to brainstorm ideas that all connected to a common problem. This helped me to narrow down my focus. Before submitting my proposal in 2019, I welcomed a second committee member, a Caucasian woman who also believed in my research.

Together, my Dissertation Chair and committee member began more frequent exchanges as I became closer to receiving approval of my Proposal. COVID-19 hit South Korea in 2019-2020, creating a domino effect in my communication with my committee. At the time, my family and I were also preparing to relocate to West Point. In 2020, after returning to the United States, it seemed like everything was off, but I remained in contact with my Dissertation Chair. She was always motivating and positive about making it to the end and walking away with my PhD. I appreciated her support and the support of my family more than anything. It took a village to keep me focused, grounded, and constantly moving toward success. Most importantly, God's grace kept me mentally and spiritually well.

I had to take a temporary military leave of absence from Walden so that I could attend Columbia Teacher's College to teach at West Point. I was devastated at first, but it was Jonathan who laid out the cards for me. "How are you losing?" "You're getting an Ivy League Degree that the Army is paying for, and you are taking a mental break from your PhD." He had a good point. I was only freaking out because July of 2020 is when I began taking a class towards my master's at Columbia. I communicated the break with my Dissertation Chair, and thank God, she was still with Walden when I returned in the summer of 2021, right after graduating from Columbia and burying my father. Yes, I went right back to working on my dissertation requirements. During the year I was off, I did not work at all with my Dissertation Chair, but I did work with Dr. KD. He was a retired Sergeant Major, with a PhD, who worked at a different college as a Diversity, Equity, and Inclusion Coordinator. I served with Dr. KD in Korea, and he told me then that he was finishing his degree and retiring after Korea. His story is incredible as well.

Dr. KD introduced me to other PhDs in my realm and discipline. I gained keen insight into how to complete and tailor my research to the civilian enterprise, not just military personnel. His efforts were the icing on the cake. I took the knowledge shared with me and continued to work with my Dissertation Chair and committee. My Proposal went back and forth to the University Research Reviewer (URR) for months before going to the Institutional Review Board (IRB). I conducted an oral presentation to the Objective Research, Scope, and Analysis Board (ORSA) for my Proposal. By April of 2022, my Proposal was complete. I began to work with my committee on submitting my completed research to the IRB. The IRB process took months.

I ended 2022 with a new desire to complete my PhD. I was so close. It seemed like things kept happening or timing with my committee, and I was off sometimes. Overall, I was frustrated leaving 2022 and not getting the results I wanted. However, I went into 2023 determined to be Dr. Jeremia Van. After all, 2023 was a good year, regardless of how you look at it. In 2023, we found out that we would return to South Korea to take Battalion Command. In 2023, I began a draft of this book. In 2023, we went to Canada for Jonathan's birthday and celebrated our grandson Caiden's birth.

January was a full month for our family! I took a quick breather and tackled February 2023 relentlessly to get approval for Form and Style, URR Final Study approval, and hopefully, get my Oral Defense scheduled. On February 1, 2023, I began to work on all of the things I just mentioned. On February 25, 2023, I successfully defended my Dissertation! God is good! All the time! And all the time! God is good! The rest involved completing the final edits for publishing and submitting them to ProQuest. My work is in the Congress National Library as well as on ProQuest. May 2023 is what my transcript says because that was the official end of the quarter! I elected to walk across the stage in July 2023! What a great way to kick off 2023 and to continue celebrating throughout that time.

I never gave up. I was often depressed, disappointed, and frustrated with myself, but when I learned to give myself some grace and focus on the "now," that's when I was able to regain what I needed to finish. I had been humble way too long. I have no idea why I let people treat me any type of way or talk to me as they see fit, and why I never told them how I felt. I have no idea why I remained extremely humble to the point where I was comfortable letting people dismiss my accomplishments, dismiss me, or continue to treat me the way they wanted in order to make themselves look good. I had gone through life changes. I had battled depression and anxiety, and won! I had to understand that what Mia wants and who Mia is should always matter to Mia. It took me almost 30 years to realize that I matter just as much as the next person. My husband, my love, my rock, Jonathan Van, has been with me on my self-love journey. He knows and appreciates me for me. I am so thankful that God saw fit to bless us with one another. I am Lieutenant Colonel Jeremia Van, PhD., and I have been too humble too long.

A Word From the Author

In the military, it is hard at times to explain things to your family and friends. However, every Soldier has a story to tell. I hope this book inspires another Soldier to tell their story. The main reason I authored this book was for my children to understand me more as a mother, a wife, a woman, and a leader. I suffered in silence for an extended period of time. It took years for me to realize who I am, and that I am worthy, not worthless. I let anxiety, depression, guilt, and low self-esteem lay dormant in my mind for way too long. I hid some of the lowest points in my life behind a smile and my work ethic. It was by the grace of God that I was able to press on. Learning and understanding the power of prayer, while cultivating a relationship with God is what saved me. When I began to see clearly, I let old habits go. When I began to see clearly, I let some friends go. When I began to see clearly, I began to hold myself accountable of how I let people treat me. I learned how to say no.

I am who God says that I am, not what the world tried to portray that I am. When you begin to grow in your faith, people that you have known all your life, often do not grow with you. If they cannot grow with you, then they cannot go with you. No longer will my past have strongholds over me. God is within me. With Him, all things are possible. I am confident. I am blessed. I am me. I hope you enjoyed *Too Humble, Too Long*.

Lieutenant Colonel Van's Assignments

2000-2006: Petroleum Supply Specialist, 894 th Quartermaster

Company, Jackson,
Mississippi
2006-2006: LDAC Lanes Operator: Fort Lewis, Washington, Officer's Basic Course,
Fort Gregg-Adams, Virginia
2006-2008: Forward Support Company, Platoon Leader and Executive Officer, Fort
Stewart, Georgia (Deployed to Iraq 2007-2008)-Served as Field Ordering Officer, Mayor Cell Deputy, Convoy Ground Commander
2009-2010: Captain's Career Course, Fort Gregg-Adams, Virginia
2010-2012: Support Operations Deputy, Distribution Company Commander in Fires
Brigade, Brigade S4, Fort Cavazos, Texas
2012: Assistant Brigade S4, Camp Shelby, MS
2012-2013: (Deployed) Senior Logistics Advisor to Afghan National Army and Afghan
National Police, Kabul, Afghanistan
2013-2016: Observer Coach Trainer, Brigade Logistics Planner, Brigade Chief of
Operations, Fort Knox, Kentucky
2016-2017: Command & General Staff College Student, Fort Leavenworth, Kansas
2017-2018: Current Operations Battle Major (S3) on General's Staff, Daegu South
Korea
2018-2019: Battalion Executive Officer, Daegu South Korea
2019-2020: Battalion Operations Officer (S3), Daegu South Korea
2020-2021: Advanced Civil Schooling (ACS); Columbia University, Teacher's College;
Master of Arts in Higher & Postsecondary Education
2021-2023: Department of Military Instruction, MS100 Instructor,

DMI S4

2023: Battalion Command Principle Select for CSL, completed PhD in Management w/

Concentration in Leadership and Organizational Change

2024-2026: Battalion Commander at DLA Energy in South Korea

Lieutenant Colonel Van's Awards & Medals

The Bronze Star Medal

Meritorious Service Medal

Army Commendation Medal

Army Achievement Medal

National Defense Service Medal

Afghanistan Campaign Medal

Iraq Campaign Medal

Global War on Terrorism Medal

Armed Forces Reserve Medal

The Army Service Ribbon

NATO Medal

Order of Saint Christopher

Education Background

2006: Bachelor's Degree, English and Modern Language, Jackson State University

2010: Master's degree in business administration, University of Phoenix

2019: Master's degree in philosophy, Walden University

2021: Master of Arts Degree in Higher Post Secondary Education, Columbia University

2023: Doctoral Degree in Management with a Concentration in Leadership and

Organizational Change, Walden University